Nothing But the Truth

by Isham, Frederic Stewart, 1866-1922

ISBN: 9781318072156

Copyright © 2016 by HardPress

HardPress
8345 NW 66TH ST #2561
MIAMI FL 33166-2626
USA
Email: info@hardpress.net

Ordering Information:

Quantity sales. Special discounts are available on quantity purchases by corporations, associations, and others. For details, contact the publisher by email at the address above.

Printed in the United States of America, United Kingdom and Australia

NOTHING BUT THE TRUTH

By

FREDERIC S. ISHAM

Author of
The Strollers, Under the Rose,
The Social Buccaneer, Etc.

INDIANAPOLIS
THE BOBBS-MERRILL COMPANY
PUBLISHERS

PRESS OF
BRAUNWORTH & CO.
BOOKBINDERS AND PRINTERS
BROOKLYN, N. Y.

Table of Contents

NOTHING BUT THE TRUTH

CHAPTER I—THE TEMERITY OF BOB

"It can't be done."

"Of course, it can."

"A man couldn't survive the ordeal."

"Could do it myself."

The scene was the University Club. The talk spread over a good deal of space, as talk will when pink cocktails, or "green gardens in a glass" confront, or are in front of, the talkees. Dickie said it couldn't be done and Bob said it was possible and that he could do it. He might not have felt such confidence had it not been for the verdant stimulation. He could have done anything just then, so why not this particular feat or stunt? And who was this temerarious one and what was he like?

As an excellent specimen of a masculine young animal, genus homo, Bob Bennett was good to look on. Some of those young ladies who wave banners when young men strain their backs and their arms and their legs in the cause of learning, had, in the days of the not remote past, dubbed him, sub rosa, the "blue-eyed Apollo." Some of the fellows not so euphemistically inclined had, however, during that same glorious period found frequent occasion to refer to him less classically, if more truthfully, as "that darn fool, Bob Bennett." That was on account of a streak of wildness in him, for he was a free bold creature, was Bob. Conventional bars and gates chafed him. He may have looked like a "blue-eyed Apollo," but his spirit had the wings of a wild goose, than which there are no faster birds—for a wild goose is the biplane of the empyrean.

Now that Bob had ceased the chase for learning and was out in the wide world, he should have acquired an additional sobriquet—that of "Impecunious Bob." It would have fitted his pecuniary condition very nicely. Once he had had great expectations, but alas!—dad had just "come a cropper." They had sheared him on the street. The world in general didn't know about it yet, but Bob did.

"We're broke, Bob," said dad that very morning.

"That's all right, Gov.," said Bob. "Can you get up?"

"I can't even procure a pair of crutches to hobble with," answered dad.

"Never mind," observed Bob magnanimously. "You've done pretty well by me up to date. Don't you worry or reproach yourself. I'm not going to heap abuse on those gray hairs."

"Thanks, Bob." Coolly. "*I'm* not worrying. You see, it's up to you now."

"Me?" Bob stared.

"Yes. You see I believe in the Japanese method."

"What's that?" Uneasily.

"Duty of a child to support his parent, when said child is grown up!"

Bob whistled. "Say, Gov., do you mean it?"

"Gospel truth, Bob."

Bob whistled again. "Not joking?"

"'Pon honor!" Cheerfully.

"I never did like the Japanese," from Bob, sotto voce. "Blame lot of heathens—that's what they are!"

"I've got a dollar or two that I owe tucked away where no one can find it except me," went on dad, unmindful of Bob's little soliloquy. "That will have to last until you come to the rescue."

"Gee! I'm glad you were thoughtful enough for that!" ejaculated the young man. "Sure you can keep it hidden?"

"Burglars couldn't find it," said dad confidently, "let alone my creditors—God bless them! But it won't last long, Bob. Bear that in mind. It'll be a mighty short respite."

"Oh, I'll not forget it. If—if it's not an impertinence, may I ask what *you* are going to do, dad?"

"I'm contemplating a fishing trip, first of all, and after that—quien sabe? Some pleasure suitable to my retired condition will undoubtedly suggest itself. I may take up the study of philosophy. Confucius has always interested me. They say it takes forty years to read him and then forty years to digest what you have read. The occupation would, no doubt, prove adequate. But don't concern yourself about that, dear boy. I'll get on. You owe me a large debt of gratitude. I'm thrusting a great responsibility on you. It should be the making of you." Bob had his secret doubts. "Get out and hustle, dear boy. It's up to you, now!" And he spread out his hands in care-free fashion and smiled blandly. No Buddha could have appeared more complacent—only instead of a lotus flower, Bob's dad held in his hand a long black weed, the puffing of which seemed to afford a large measure of ecstatic satisfaction. "Go!" He waved the free hand. "My blessing on your efforts."

Bob started to go, and then he lingered. "Perhaps," he said, "you can tell me *what* I am going to do?"

"Don't know." Cheerfully.

"What *can* I do?" Hopelessly.

"Couldn't say."

"I don't know *anything*."

"Ha! ha!" Dad laughed, as if son had sprung a joke. "Well, that is a condition experience will remove. Experience *and* hard knocks," he added.

Bob swore softly. His head was humming. No heroic purpose to get out and fight his way moved him. He didn't care about shoveling earth, or chopping down trees. He had no frenzied desire to brave the sixty-below-zero temperature of the Klondike in a mad search for gold. In a word, he didn't feel at all like the heroes in the books who conquer under almost impossible conditions in the vastnesses of the "open," and incidentally whallop a few herculean simple-minded sons of nature, just to prove that breed is better than brawn.

"Of course, I could give you a little advice, Bob," said the governor softly. "If you should find hustling a bit arduous for one of your luxurious nature, there's an alternative. It is always open to a young man upon whom nature has showered her favors."

"Don't know what you mean by that last," growled Bob, who disliked personalities. "But what is the alternative to hustling?"

"Get married," said dad coolly.

Bob changed color. Dad watched him keenly.

"There's always the matrimonial market for young men who have not learned to specialize. I've known many such marriages to turn out happily, too. Marrying right, my boy, is a practical, not a sentimental business."

Bob looked disgusted.

"There's Miss Gwendoline Gerald, for example. Millions in her own name, and—"

"Hold on, dad!" cried Bob. His face was flaming now. The blue eyes gleamed almost fiercely.

"I knew you were acquainted," observed dad softly, still studying him. "Besides she's a beautiful girl and—"

"Drop it, dad!" burst from Bob. "We've never had a quarrel, but—" Suddenly he realized his attitude was actually menacing. And toward dad—his own dad! "I beg your pardon, sir," he muttered contritely. "I'm afraid I am forgetting myself. But please turn the talk."

"All right," said dad. "I forgive you. I was only trying to elucidate your position. But since it's not to be the matrimonial market, it'll have to be a hustle, my boy. I'm too old to make another fortune. I've done my bit and now I'm going to retire on my son. Sounds fair and equitable, doesn't it, Bob?"

"I'd hate to contradict you, sir," the other answered moodily.

Dad walked up to him and laid an arm affectionately upon son's broad shoulders. "I've the utmost confidence in you, my boy," he said, with a bland smile.

"Thank you, sir," replied Bob. He always preserved an attitude of filial respect toward his one and only parent. But he tore himself away from dad now as soon as he could. He wanted to think. The average hero, thrust out into the world, has only a single load to carry. He has only to earn a living for himself. Bob's load was a double one and therefore he would have to be a double hero. Mechanically he walked on and on, cogitating upon his unenviable fate. Suddenly he stopped. He found himself in front of the club. Bob went in. And there he met Dickie, Clarence, Dan the doughty "commodore" and some others.

That Impecunious Bob should have said "It could be done" to Imperial Dickie's "It couldn't" and have allowed himself to be drawn further into the affair was, in itself, an impertinence. For Dickie was a person of importance. He had a string of simoleons so long that a newspaper-mathematician once computed if you spread them out, touching one another, they would reach half around the world. Or was it twice around? Anyhow, Dickie didn't have to worry about hustling, the way Bob did now. At the moment the latter was in a mood to contradict any one. He felt reckless. He was ready for almost anything—short of an imitation of that back-to-nature hero of a popular novel.

They had been going on about that "could" and "couldn't" proposition for some time when some one staked Bob. That some one was promptly "called" by the "commodore"—as jolly a sea-dog as never trod a deck. Dan was a land-commodore, but he was very popular at the Yacht Club, where something besides waves seethed when he was around. He didn't go often to the University Club where he complained things were too pedagogic. (No one else ever complained of that.) He liked to see the decks—or floors—wave.

Then he was in his element and would issue orders with the blithe abandon of a son of Neptune. There was no delay in "clapping on sail" when the commodore was at the helm. And if he said: "Clear the decks for action," there was action. When he did occasionally drift into the University, he brought with him the flavor of the sea. Things at once breezed up.

Well, the commodore called that some one quick.

"Five thousand he can't do it."

"For how long?" says Dickie.

"A week," answered the commodore.

"Make it two."

"Oh, very well."

"Three, if you like!" from Bob, the stormy petrel.

They gazed at him admiringly.

"It isn't the green garden talking, is it, Bob?" asked Clarence Van Duzen whose sole occupation was being a director in a few corporations—or, more strictly speaking, *not* being one. It took almost all Clarence's time to "direct" his wife, or try to.

Bob looked at Clarence reproachfully. "No," he said. "I'm still master of all my thoughts." Gloomily. "I couldn't forget if I tried."

"That's all right, then," said Dickie.

Then Clarence "took" some one else who staked Bob. And Dickie did likewise. And there was some more talk. And then Bob staked himself.

"Little short of cash at the bank just now," he observed. "But if you'll take my note—"

"Take your word if you want," said the commodore.

"No; here's my note." He gave it—a large amount—payable in thirty days. It was awful, but he did it. He hardly thought what he was doing. Having the utmost confidence he would win, he didn't stop to realize what a large contract he was taking on. But Dan, Dickie, Clarence and the others did.

"Of course, you can't go away and hide," said Dickie to Bob with sudden suspicion.

"No; you can't do that," from Clarence. "Or get yourself arrested and locked up for three weeks! That wouldn't be fair, old chap."

"Bob understands he's got to go on in the even tenor of his way," said the commodore.

Bob nodded. "Just as if nothing had happened!" he observed. "I'll not seek, or I'll not shirk. I'm on honor, you understand."

"That's good enough for me!" said Dickie. "Bob's honest."

"And me!" from Clarence.

"And me!" from half a dozen other good souls, including the non-aqueous commodore.

"Gentlemen, I thank you," said Bob, affected by this outburst of confidence. "I thank you for this display of—this display—"

"Cut it!"

"Cork it up! And speaking of corks—"

"When does it begin?" interrupted Bob.

"When you walk out of here,"

"At the front door?"

"When your foot touches the sidewalk, son." The commodore who was about forty in years sometimes assumed the paternal.

"Never mind the 'son.'" Bob shuddered. "One father at a time, please!" And then hastily, not to seem ungracious: "I've got such a jolly good, real dad, you understand—"

The commodore dropped the paternal. "Well, lads, here's a bumper to Bob," he said.

"We see his finish."

"No doubt of that."

"To Bob! Good old Bob! Ho! ho!"

"Ha! ha!" said Bob funereally.

Then he got up.

"Going?"

"Might as well."

The commodore drew out a watch.

"Twelve minutes after three p.m. Monday, the twelfth of September, in the year of our Lord, 1813," he said. "You are all witnesses of the time the ball was opened?"

"We are."

"Good-by, Bob."

"Oh, let's go with him a way!"

"*Might* be interesting," from Clarence sardonically.

"It might. Least we can do is to see him start on his way rejoicing."

"That's so. Come on." Which they did.

Bob offered no objection. He didn't much care at the time whether they did or not. What would happen would. He braced himself for the inevitable.

CHAPTER II—A TRY-OUT

To tell the truth—to blurt out nothing but the truth to every one, and on every occasion, for three whole weeks—that's what Bob had contracted to do. From the point of view of the commodore and the others, the man who tried to fill this contract would certainly be shot, or electrocuted, or ridden out of town on a rail, or receive a coat of tar and feathers. And Bob had such a wide circle of friends, too, which would make his task the harder; the handsome dog was popular. He was asked everywhere that was anywhere and he went, too. He would certainly "get his." The jovial commodore was delighted. He would have a whole lot of fun at Bob's expense. Wasn't the latter the big boob, though? And wouldn't he be put through his paces? Really it promised to be delicious. The commodore and the others went along with Bob just for a little try-out.

At first nothing especially interesting happened. They walked without meeting any one they were acquainted with. Transients! transients! where did they all come from? Once on their progress down the avenue the hopes of Bob's friends rose high. A car they knew got held up on a side street not far away from them. It was a gorgeous car and it had a gorgeous occupant, but a grocery wagon was between them and it. The commodore warbled blithely.

"Come on, Bob. Time for a word or two!"

But handsome Bob shook his head. "The 'even tenor of his way,'" he quoted. "I don't ordinarily go popping in and out between wheels like a rabbit. I'm not looking to commit suicide."

"Oh, I only wanted to say: 'How do you do,'" retorted the commodore rather sulkily. "Or 'May I tango with you at tea this afternoon, Mrs. Ralston?'"

"Or observe: 'How young she looks to-day, eh, Bob?'" murmured that young gentleman suspiciously.

"Artful! Artful!" Clarence poked the commodore in the ribs. "Sly old sea-dog!"

"Well, let's move on," yawned Dickie. "Nothing doing here."

"Wait!" The commodore had an idea. "Hi, you young grocery lad, back up a little, will you?"

"Wha' for?" said the boy, aggressive at once. Babes are born in New York with chips on their shoulders.

"As a matter of trifling accommodation, that is all," answered the commodore sweetly. "On the other side of you is a stately car and we would hold conversation with—"

"Aw, gwan! Guess I got as much right to the street as it has." And as a display of his "rights," he even touched up his horse a few inches, to intervene more thoroughly.

"Perhaps now for half a dollar—" began the commodore, more insinuatingly. Then he groaned: "Too late!" The policeman had lifted the ban. The stately car turned into the avenue and was swallowed up amid a myriad of more or less imposing vehicles. They had, however, received a bow from the occupant. That was all there had been opportunity for. Incidentally, the small boy had bestowed upon them his parting compliments:

"Smart old guy! You think youse—" The rest was jumbled up or lost in the usual cacophony of the thoroughfare.

"Too bad!" murmured the commodore. "But still these three weeks are young."

"'Three weeks!'" observed Dickie. "Sounds like plagiarism!"

"Oh, Bob won't have that kind of a 'three weeks,'" snickered Clarence.

"Bob's will be an expurgated edition," from the commodore, recovering his spirits.

"Maybe we ought to make it four?"

"Three will do," said Bob, who wasn't enjoying this chaffing. Every one they approached he now eyed apprehensively.

But he was a joy-giver, if not receiver, for his tall handsome figure attracted many admiring glances. His striking head with its blond curls—they weren't exactly curls, only his hair wasn't straight, but clung rather wavy-like to the bold contour of his head—his careless stride, and that general effect of young masculinity—all this caused sundry humble feminine hearts to go pit-a-pat. Bob's progress, however, was generally followed by pit-a-pats from shop-girls and bonnet-bearers. Especially at the noon hour! Then Bob seemed to these humble toilers, like dessert, after hard-boiled eggs, stale sandwiches and pickles.

But Bob was quite unaware of any approving glances cast after him. He was thinking, and thinking hard. He wasn't so sanguine now as he had been when he had left the club. What might have happened at that street corner appealed to him with sudden poignant force. Mrs. Ralston was of the *creme de la creme*. She was determined to stay young. She pretended to be thirty years or so younger than she was. In fact, she was rather a ridiculous old lady who found it hard to conceal her age. Now what if the commodore had found opportunity to ask that awful question? Bob could have made only one reply and told the truth. The largeness of his contract was becoming more apparent to him. He began to see himself now from Dan's standpoint. Incidentally, he was beginning to develop a great dislike for that genial land-mariner.

"How about the Waldorf?" They had paused at the corner of Thirty-fourth Street. "May find some one there," suggested Clarence.

"In Peek-a-Boo Alley?" scornfully from Dickie.

"Oh, I heard there was a concert, or something upstairs," said Clarence. "In that you've-got-to-be-introduced room! And some of the real people have to walk through to get to it."

Accordingly they entered the Waldorf and the commodore hustled them up and down and around, without, however, their encountering a single "real" person. There were only people present—loads of them, not from somewhere but from everywhere. They did the circuit several times, still without catching sight of a real person.

"Whew! This *is* a lonesome place!" breathed the commodore at last.

"Let's depart!" disgustedly from Clarence. "Apologize for steering you into these barren wastes!"

"What's your hurry?" said Bob, with a little more bravado. Then suddenly he forgot about those other three. His entranced gaze became focused on one. He saw only her.

"Ha!" The commodore's quick glance, following Bob's, caught sight, too, of that wonderful face in the distance—the stunning, glowing young figure—that regal dream of just-budded girlhood—that superb vision in a lovely afternoon gown! She was followed by one or two others. One could only imagine her leading. There would, of course, always be several at her either side and quite a number dangling behind. Her lips were like the red rosebuds that swung negligently from her hand as she floated through the crowd. Her eyes suggested veiled dreams amid the confusion and hubbub of a topsyturvy world. She was like something rhythmical precipitated amid chaos. A far-away impression of a smile played around the corners of her proud lips.

The commodore precipitated himself in her direction. Bob put out a hand as if to grasp him by the coat tails, but the other was already beyond reach and Bob's hand fell to his side. He stood passive. That was his part. Only he wasn't passive inwardly. His heart was beating wildly. He could imagine himself with her and them—those others in her train—and the conversation that would ensue, for he had no doubt of the commodore's intentions. Dan was an adept at rounding up people. Bob could see himself at a table participating in the conversation—prepared conversation, some of it! He could imagine the commodore leading little rivulets of talk into certain channels for his benefit. Dan would see to it that they would ask him (Bob) questions, embarrassing ones. That "advice" dad had given him weighed on Bob like a nightmare. Suppose—ghastly thought!—

truth compelled him ever to speak of that? And to her! A shiver ran down Bob's backbone. Nearer she drew—nearer—while Bob gazed as if fascinated, full of rapturous, paradoxical dread. Now the commodore was almost upon her when—

Ah, what was that? An open elevator?—people going in?—She, too,—those with her—Yes—click! a closed door! The radiant vision had vanished, was going upward; Bob breathed again. Think of being even paradoxically glad at witnessing *her* disappear! Bob ceased now to think; stood as in a trance.

"Why *do* people go to concerts?" said the commodore in aggrieved tones. "Some queen, that!"

"And got the rocks—or stocks!" from Dickie. "Owns about three of those railroads that are going a-begging nowadays."

"Wake up, Bobbie!" some one now addressed that abstracted individual.

Bob shook himself.

"Old friend of yours, Miss Gwendoline Gerald, I believe?" said the commodore significantly.

"Yes; I've known Miss Gerald for some time," said Bob coldly.

"'Known for some time'—" mimicked the commodore. "Phlegmatic dog! Well, what shall we do now?"

"Hang around until the concert's over?" suggested Dickie.

"Hang around nothing!" said the commodore. "It's one of those classical high-jinks." Disgustedly. "Lasts so late the sufferers haven't time for anything after it's over. Just enough energy left to stagger to their cars and fall over in a comatose condition."

"Suppose we *could* go to the bar?"

"Naughty! Naughty!" A sprightly voice interrupted.

The commodore wheeled. "Mrs. Ralston!" he exclaimed gladly.

It was the gorgeous lady of the gorgeous car.

"Just finished my shopping and thought I'd have a look in here," she said vivaciously.

"Concert, I suppose?" from the commodore, jubilantly.

"Yes. Dubussy. Don't you adore Dubussy?" with schoolgirlish enthusiasm. Though almost sixty, she had the manners of a "just-come-out."

"Nothing like it," lied the commodore.

"Ah, then you, too, are a modern?" gushed the lady.

"I'm so advanced," said the commodore, "I can't keep up with myself."

They laughed. "Ah, silly man!" said the lady's eyes. Bob gazed at her and the commodore enviously. Oh, to be able once more to prevaricate like that! The commodore had never heard Dubussy in his life. Ragtime and merry hornpipes were his limits. And Mrs. Ralston was going to the concert, it is true, but to hear the music? Ah, no! Her box was a fashionable rendezvous, and from it she could study modernity in hats. Therein, at least, she was a modern of the moderns. She was so advanced, the styles had fairly to trot, or turkey-trot, to keep up with her.

"Well," she said, with that approving glance women usually bestowed upon Bob, "I suppose I mustn't detain you busy people after that remark I overheard."

"Oh, don't hurry," said the commodore hastily. "Between old friends— But I say— By jove, you *are* looking well. Never saw you looking so young and charming. Never!" It was rather crudely done, but the commodore could say things more bluntly than other people and "get away with them." He was rather a privileged character. Bob began to breathe hard, having a foretaste of what was to follow. And Mrs. "Willie" Ralston was Miss Gwendoline Gerald's aunt! No doubt that young lady was up in her aunt's box at this moment.

"Never!" repeated the commodore. "Eh, Bob? Doesn't look a day over thirty," with a jovial, freehearted sailor laugh. "Does she now?"

It had come. That first test! And the question had to be answered. The lady was looking at Bob. They were all waiting. A fraction of a second, or so, which seemed like a geological epoch, Bob hesitated. He had to reply and yet being a gentleman, how could he? No matter what it cost him, he would simply have to "lie like a gentleman." He—

Suddenly an idea shot through his befuddled brain. Maybe Mrs. Ralston wouldn't know what he said, if he—? She had been numerous times to France, of course, but she was not mentally a heavy-weight. Languages might not be her forte. Presumably she had all she could do to chatter in English. Bob didn't know much French himself. He would take a chance on her, however. He made a bow which was Chesterfieldian and incidentally made answer, rattling it off with the swiftness of a boulevardier.

"*Il me faut dire que, vraiment, Madame Ralston parait aussi agee qu'elle l'est!*" ("I am obliged to say that Mrs. Ralston appears as old as she is!")

Then he straightened as if he had just delivered a stunning compliment.

"*Merci!*" The lady smiled. She also beamed. "How well you speak French, Mr. Bennett!"

The commodore nearly exploded. *He* understood French.

Bob expanded, beginning to breathe freely once more. "Language of courtiers and diplomats!" he mumbled.

Mrs. Ralston shook an admonishing finger at him. "Flatterer!" she said, and departed.

Whereupon the commodore leaned weakly against Dickie while Clarence sank into a chair. First round for Bob!

The commodore was the first to recover. His voice was reproachful. "Was *that* quite fair?—that parleyvoo business? I don't know about it's being allowed."

"Why not?" calmly from Bob. "Is truth confined to one tongue?"

"But what about that 'even tenor of your way'?" fenced the commodore. "You don't, as a usual thing, go around parleyvooing—"

"What about the even tenor of your own ways?" retorted Bob.

"Nothing said about *that* when we—"

"No, but—how can *I* go the even tenor, if *you* don't go yours?"

"Hum?" said the commodore.

"Don't you see it's not the even tenor?" persisted Bob. "But it's your fault if it isn't."

"Some logic in that," observed Clarence.

"Maybe, we *have* been a bit too previous," conceded the commodore.

"That isn't precisely the adjective I would use," returned Bob. He found himself thinking more clearly now. They had all, perhaps, been stepping rather lightly when they had left the club. He should have thought of this before. But Bob's brain moved rather slowly sometimes and the others had been too bent on having a good time to consider all the ethics of the case. They showed themselves fair-minded enough now, however.

"Bob's right," said the commodore sorrowfully. "Suppose we've got to eliminate ourselves from his agreeable company for the next three weeks, unless we just naturally happen to meet. We'll miss a lot of fun, but I guess it's just got to be. What about that parleyvooing business though, Bob?"

"That's got to be eliminated, too!" from Dickie. "Why, he might tell the truth in Chinese."

"All right, fellows," said Bob shortly. "You quit tagging and I'll talk United States."

"Good. I'm off," said the commodore. And he went. The others followed. Bob was left alone. He found the solitude blessed and began to have hopes once more. Why, he might even be permitted to enjoy a real lonely three weeks, now that he had got rid of that trio. He drew out a cigar and began to tell himself he *was* enjoying himself when—

"Mr. Robert Bennett!" The voice of a page smote the air. It broke into his reflections like a shock.

"Mr. Bennett!" again bawled the voice.

For the moment Bob was tempted to let him slip by, but conscience wouldn't let him. He lifted a finger.

"Message for Mr. Bennett," said the urchin.

Bob took it. He experienced forebodings as he saw the dainty card and inscription. He read it. Then he groaned. Would Mr. Robert Bennett join Mrs. Ralston's house-party at Tonkton? There were a few more words in that impulsive lady's characteristic, vivacious style. And then there were two words in another handwriting that he knew. "Will you?" That "Will you?" wasn't signed. Bob stared at it. Would he? He had to. He was in honor bound, because ordinarily he would have accepted with alacrity. But a house-party for him, under present circumstances! He would be a merry guest. Ye gods and little fishes! And then some! He gave a hollow laugh, while the urchin gazed at him sympathetically. Evidently the gentleman had received bad news.

CHAPTER III—AN INAUSPICIOUS BEGINNING

Mrs. Ralston's house-parties were usually satisfactory affairs. She was fond of people, especially young people, and more especially of young men of the Apollo variety, though in a strictly proper, platonic and critical sense. Indeed, her taste in the abstract, for animated Praxiteles had, for well-nigh two-score of years, been unimpeachable. At the big gatherings in her noble country mansion, there was always a liberal sprinkling of decorative and animated objects of art of this description. She liked to ornament her porches or her gardens with husky and handsome young college athletes. She had an intuitive artistic taste for stunning living-statuary, "dressed up," of course. Bob came distinctly in that category. So behold him then, one fine morning, on the little sawed-off train that whisked common people—and sometimes a few notables when their cars were otherwise engaged—countryward. Bob had a big grip by his side, his golf sticks were in a rack and he had a newspaper in his hand. The sunshine came in on him but his mood was not sunny. An interview with dad just before leaving hadn't improved his spirits. He had found dad at the breakfast table examining a book of artificial flies, on one hand, and a big reel on the other.

"Which shall it be, my son?" dad had greeted him cordially. "Trout or tarpon?"

"I guess that's for you to decide," Robert had answered grumpily. Dad, in his new role, was beginning to get on Bob's nerves. Dad didn't seem to be at all concerned about his future. He shifted that weighty and momentous subject just as lightly! He acted as if he hadn't a care in the world.

"Wish I *could* make up my mind," he said, like a boy in some doubt how he can best put in his time when he plays hooky. "Minnows or whales? I'll toss up." He did. "Whales win. By the way, how's the hustling coming on?"

"Don't know."

"Well, don't put it off too long." Cheerfully. "I guess I can worry along for about three weeks."

"Three weeks!" said Bob gloomily. Oh, that familiar sound!

"You wouldn't have me stint myself, would you, my son?" Half reproachfully. "You wouldn't have dad deny himself anything?"

"No," answered the other truthfully enough. As a matter of fact things couldn't be much worse, so he didn't much care. Fortunately, dad didn't ask any questions or show any curiosity about that "hustling" business. He seemed to take it for granted Bob would arise to the occasion and be as indulgent a son as he had been an indulgent dad—for he had never denied the boy anything. Bob softened when he thought of that. But confound dad's childlike faith in him, at this period of emergency. It made Bob nervous. He had no faith in himself that way. Dad *did* lift his eyebrows just a little when Bob brought down his big grip.

"Week-end?" he hazarded.

"Whole week," replied Bob in a melancholy tone.

"Whither?"

"Tonkton."

Dad beamed. "Mrs. Ralston?"

"Yes."

"Aunt of Miss Gwendoline Gerald, I believe?" With a quick penetrating glance at Bob.

"Yes."

"Sensible boy," observed dad, still studying him.

"Oh, I'm not going for the reason you think," said Bob quite savagely. He was most unlike himself.

"Of course not." Dad was conciliatory.

"I'm not. Think what you like."

"Too much work to think," yawned dad.

"But you *are* thinking." Resentfully.

"Have it your own way."

Bob squared his shoulders. "You want to know really why I'm going to Tonkton?"

"Have I ever tried to force your confidences, my son?"

"I'm going because I've got to. I can't help myself."

"Of course," said dad. "Ta! ta! Enjoy yourself. See you in three weeks."

"Three—!" But Bob didn't finish. What was the use? Dad thought he was going to Tonkton because Miss Gerald might be there.

As a matter of fact Bob's one great wish now was that she wouldn't be there. He wanted, and yet didn't want, to see her. What had he to hope now? Why, he didn't have a son, or not enough of them to count. He was to all practical intents and purposes a pauper. Dad's "going broke" had changed his whole life. He had been reared in the lap of luxury, a pampered son. He had never dreamed of being otherwise. And considering himself a favored child of fortune, he had even dared entertain the delirious hope of winning her—her, the goddess of his dreams.

But hope now was gone. Regrets were useless. He could no longer conceive himself in the role of suitor. Why, there were few girls in the whole land so overburdened with "rocks"—as Dickie called them! If only she didn't have those rocks—or stocks! "Impecunious Gwendoline!" How well that would go with "Impecunious Bob!" If only her trustees would hit the toboggan, the way dad did! But trustees don't go tobogganing. They eschew the smooth and slippery. They speculate in government bonds and things that fluctuate about a point or so a century. No chance for quick action there! On the contrary, the trustees were probably making those millions grow. Bob heaved a sigh. Then he took something white from his pocket and gazed at two words, ardently yet dubiously.

That "Will you?" of hers on Mrs. Ralston's card exhilarated and at the same time depressed him. It implied she, herself, did expect to be at her aunt's country place. He attached no other especial importance to the "Will you?" An imperious young person in her exalted position could command as she pleased. She could say "Will you?" or "You will" to dozens of more or less callow youths, or young grown-ups, with impunity, and none of said dozens would attach any undue flattering meaning to her words. Miss Gerald found safety in numbers. She was as yet heart-free.

"Can you—aw!—tell me how far it is to Tonkton?" a voice behind here interrupted his ruminations.

Bob hastily returned the card to his pocket, and glancing back, saw a monocle. "Matter of ten miles or so," he responded curtly. He didn't like monocles.

"Aw!" said the man.

Bob picked up his newspaper that he had laid down, and frowningly began to glance over the head-lines. The man behind him glanced over them, too.

"Another society robbery, I see," the latter remarked. "No function complete without them nowadays, I understand. Wonderful country, America! Guests here always expect—aw!—to be robbed, I've been told."

"Have the paper," said Bob with cutting accents.

"Thanks awfully." The man with the monocle took the paper as a matter of course, seeming totally unaware of the sarcasm in Bob's tone. At first, Bob felt like kicking himself; the rustle of the paper in those alien hands caused him to shuffle his feet with mild irritation. Then he forgot all about the paper and the monocle man. His thoughts began once more to go over and over the same old ground, until—

"T'nk'n!" The stentorian abbreviation of the conductor made Bob get up with a start. Grabbing his grip—hardly any weight at all for his muscular arm—in one hand, and his implements of the game in the other, he swung down the aisle and on to the platform. A good many people got off, for a small town nestled beneath the high rolling lands of the country estates of the affluent. There were vehicles of all kinds at the station, among them a number of cars, and in one of the latter Bob recognized Mrs. Ralston's chauffeur.

A moment he hesitated. He supposed he ought to step forward and get in, for that was what he naturally would do. But he wanted to think; he didn't want to get to the house in a hurry. Still he had to do what he naturally would do and he started to do it when some other people Bob didn't know—prospective guests, presumably, among them the man with the monocle—got into the car and fairly filled it. That let Bob out nicely and naturally. It gave him another breathing spell. He had got so he was looking forward to these little breathing spells.

"Hack, sir?" said a voice.

"Not for me," replied Bob. "But you can tote this up the hill," indicating the grip. "Ralston house."

"Dollar and a half, sir," said the man. "Same price if you go along, too."

"What?" It just occurred to Bob he hadn't many dollars left, and of course, tips would be expected up there, at the big house. It behooved him, therefore, to be frugal. But to argue about a dollar and a half!—he, a guest at the several million dollar house! On the other hand, that dollar looked large to Bob at this moment. Imagine if he had to earn a dollar and a half! He couldn't at the moment tell how he would do it.

"Hold on." Bob took the grip away from the man. "Why, it's outrageous, such a tariff! Same price, with or without me, indeed! I tell you—" Suddenly he stopped. He had an awful realization that he was acting a part. That forced indignation of his was not the truth; that aloof kind of an attitude wasn't the truth, either.

"To tell you the truth," said Bob, "I can't afford it."

"Can't afford. Ha! ha!" That was a joke. One of Mrs. Ralston's guests, not afford—!

"No," said Bob. "I've only got about fifteen dollars and a half to my name. I guess you're worth more than that yourself, aren't you?" With sudden respect in his tone.

"I guess I am," said the man, grinning.

"Then, logically, I should be carrying your valise," retorted Bob.

"Ha! ha! That's good." The fellow had been transporting the overflow of Mrs. Ralston's guests for years, but he had never met quite such an eccentric one as this. He chuckled now as if it were the best joke. "I'll tell you what—I'll take it for nothing, and leave it to you what you give me!" Maybe, for a joke, he'd get a fifty— dollars, not cents. These young millionaire men did perpetrate little funnyisms like that. Why, one of them had once "beat him down" a quarter on his fare and then given him ten dollars for a tip. "Ha! ha!" repeated the fellow, surveying Bob's elegant and faultless attire, "I'll do it for nothing, and you—"

Bob walked away carrying his grip. Here he was telling the truth and he wasn't believed. The man took him for one of those irresponsible merry fellows. That was odd. Was it auspicious? Should he derive encouragement therefrom? Maybe the others would only say "Ha! ha!" when he told the truth. But though he tried to feel the fellow's attitude was a good omen, he didn't succeed very well.

No use trying to deceive *himself*! Might as well get accustomed to that truth-telling habit even in his own thoughts! That diabolical trio of friends had seen plainer than he. *They* had realized the dazzling difficulties of the task confronting him. How they were laughing in their sleeves now at "darn fool Bob!" Bob, a young Don Quixote, sallying forth to attempt the impossible! The preposterous part of the whole business was that his role *was* preposterous. Why, he really and truly, in his transformed condition, ought to be just like every one else. That he was a unique exception—a figure alone in

29| Page

his glory, or ingloriously alone—was a fine commentary on this old world, anyhow.

What an old humbug of a world it was, he thought, when, passing before the one and only book-store the little village boasted of, he ran plump into, or almost into, Miss Gwendoline Gerald.

She, at that moment, had just emerged from the shop with a supply of popular magazines in her arms. A gracious expression immediately softened the young lady's lovely patrician features and she extended a hand. As in a dream Bob looked at it, for the fraction of a second. It was a beautiful, shapely and capable hand. It was also sunburned. It looked like the hand of a young woman who would grasp what she wanted and wave aside peremptorily what she didn't want. It was a strong hand, but it was also an adorable hand. It went with the proud but lovely face. It supplemented the steady, direct violet eyes. The pink nails gleamed like sea-shells. Bob set down the grip and took the hand. His heart was going fast.

"Glad to see you," said Miss Gwendoline.

Bob remained silent. He was glad and he wasn't glad. That is to say, he was deliriously glad and he knew he ought not to be. He found it difficult to conceal the effect she had upon him. He dreaded, too, the outcome of that meeting. So, how should he answer and yet tell the truth? It was considerable of a "poser," he concluded, as he strove to collect his perturbed thoughts.

"Well, why don't you say something?" she asked.

"Lovely clay," observed Bob.

The violet eyes drilled into him slightly. Shades of Hebe! but she had a fine figure! She looked great next to Bob. Maybe she knew it. Perhaps that was why she was just a shade more friendly and gracious to him than to some of the others. They two appeared so well together. He certainly did set her off.

"Is that all you have to say?" asked Miss Gwendoline after a moment.

"Let me put those magazines in the trap for you?" said Bob, making a desperate recovery and indicating the smart rig at the curb as he spoke.

"Thanks," she answered. "Make yourself useful." And gave them to him. But there was now a slight reserve on her part. His manner had slightly puzzled her. There was a constraint, or hold-offishness about him that seemed to her rather a new symptom in him. What did it mean? Had he misinterpreted her "Will you?" The violet eyes flashed slightly, then she laughed. How ridiculous!

"There! You did it very well," she commended him mockingly.

"Thanks," said Bob awkwardly, and shifted. It would be better if she let him go. Those awful things he might say?—that she might make him say? But she showed no disposition to permit him to depart at once. She lingered. People didn't usually seek to terminate talks with her. As a rule they just stuck and stuck around and it was hard to get rid of them. Did she divine his uneasiness? Bob showed he certainly wasn't enjoying himself. The violet eyes grew more and more puzzled.

"What a brilliant conversationalist you are to-day, Mr. Bennett!" she remarked with a trace of irony in her tones.

"Yes; I don't feel very strong on the talk to-day," answered Bob truthfully.

Miss Gwendoline pondered a moment on this. She had seen young men embarrassed before—especially when she was alone with them. Sometimes her decidedly pronounced beauty had a disquieting effect on certain sensitive young souls. Bob's manner recalled the manner of one or two of those others just before they indulged, or tried to indulge, in unusual sentiments, or too close personalities. Miss Gerald's long sweeping lashes lowered ominously. Then they slowly lifted. She didn't feel to-day any inordinate endeavor or desire on Bob's part to break down the nice barriers of convention and to establish that more intimate and magnetic atmosphere of a new relationship. Well, that was the way it should be. It must be he was only stupid at the moment. That's why he acted strange and unlike himself.

Perhaps he had been up late the night before. Maybe he had a headache. His handsome face was certainly very sober. There was a silent appeal to her in that blond head, a little over half-a-head above hers. Miss Gwendoline's red lips softened. What a great, big, nice-looking boy he was, after all! She let the lights of her eyes play on him more kindly. She had always thought Bob a good sort. He was an excellent partner in tennis and when it came to horses—they had certainly had some great spurts together. She had tried to follow Bob but it had sometimes been hard. His "jumps" were famous. What he couldn't put a horse over, no one else could. For the sake of these and a few kindred recollections, she softened.

"I suppose men sometimes do feel that way the next day," she observed with tentative sympathy. One just had to forgive Bob. She knew a lot of cleverer men who weren't half so interesting on certain occasions. Intellectual conversation isn't everything. Even that soul-to-soul talk of the higher faddists sometimes palled. "I suppose that's why you're walking."

"Why?" he repeated, puzzled.

"To dissipate that 'tired feeling,' I believe you call it?"

"But I'm not tired," said Bob.

"Headachey, then?"

"No." He wasn't quite following the subtleties of her remarks.

"Then why *are* you walking?" she persisted. "And with that?" Touching his grip with the tip of her toe.

"Save hack fare," answered Bob.

She smiled.

"Man wanted a dollar and a half," he went on.

"And you objected?" Lightly.

"I did."

Again she smiled. Bob saw she, too, thought it was a joke. And he remembered how she knew of one or two occasions when he had just thrown money to the winds—shoved it out of the window, as it were—orchids, by the dozens, tips, two or three times too large, etc. Bob, with those reckless eyes, object to a dollar and a half—or a hundred and fifty, for that matter? Not he! If ever there had been a spendthrift!—

"Well, I'll lend a hand to a poor, poverty-stricken wretch," said Miss Gerald, indulgently entering into the humor of the situation.

"What do you mean?" With new misgivings.

"Put them"—indicating the grip and the sticks—"in the trap," she commanded.

Bob did. He couldn't do anything else. And then he assisted her in.

"Thanks for timely help!" he said more blithely, as he saw her slip on her gloves and begin to gather up the reins with those firm capable fingers. "And now—?" He started as if to go.

"Oh, you can get in, too." Why shouldn't he? There was room for two. She spoke in a matter-of-fact manner.

"I—?" Bob hesitated. A long, long drive—unbounded opportunity for chats, confidences!—and all at the beginning of his sojourn here? Dad's words—that horrid advice—burned on his brain like fire. He tried to think of some excuse for not getting in. He might say he had to stop at a drug store, or call up a man in New York on business by telephone, or— But no! he couldn't say any of those things. He was denied the blissful privilege of other men.

"Well, why don't you get in?" Miss Gerald spoke more sharply. "Don't you want to?"

The words came like a thunder-clap, though Miss Gwendoline's voice was honey sweet. Bob raised a tragic head. That monster, Truth!

"No," he said.

An instant Miss Gwendoline looked at him, the violet eyes incredulous, amused. Then a slight line appeared on her beautiful forehead and her red lips parted a little as if she were going to say something, but didn't. Instead, they closed tight, the way rosebuds shut when the night is unusually frosty. Her eyes became hard like diamonds.

"How charmingly frank!" she said. Then she drew up the reins and trailed the tip of the whip caressingly along the back of her spirited cob. It sprang forward. "Look out for the sun, Mr. Bennett," she called back as they dashed away. "It's rather hot to-day."

Bob stood and stared after her. What did she mean about the sun? Did she think he had a touch of sunstroke, or brain-fever? It was an inauspicious beginning, indeed. If he had only known what next was coming!

CHAPTER IV—A CHAT ON THE LINKS

At the top of the hill, instead of following the winding road, Bob started leisurely across the rolling green toward the big house whose roof could be discerned in the distance above the trees. The day was charming, but he was distinctly out of tune. There was a frown on his brow. Fate had gone too far. He half-clenched his fists, for he was in a fighting mood and wanted to retaliate—but how? At the edge of some bushes he came upon a lady—no less a personage than the better-half of the commodore, himself.

She was fair, fat and forty, or a little more. She was fooling with a white ball, or rather it was fooling with her, for she didn't seem to like the place where it lay. She surveyed it from this side and then from that. To the casual observer it looked just the same from whichever point you viewed it. Once or twice the lady, evidently no expert, raised her arm and then lowered it. But apparently, at last, she made up her mind. She was just about to hit the little ball, though whether to top or slice it will never be known, when Bob stepped up from behind the bushes.

"Oh, Mr. Bennett!" He had obviously startled her.

"The same," said Bob gloomily.

"That's too bad of you," she chided him, stepping back.

"What?"

"Why, I'd just got it all figured out in my mind how to do it."

"Sorry," said Bob. "I didn't know you were behind the bushes or I wouldn't have come out on you like that. But maybe you'll do even better than you were going to. Hope so! Go ahead with your drive. Don't mind me." His tone was depressed, if not sepulchral.

But the lady, being at that sociable age, showed now a perverse disposition not to "go ahead."

"Just get here?" she asked.

"Yes. Anything doing?"

"Not much. It's been, in fact, rather slow. Mrs. Ralston says so herself. So I am at liberty to make the same remark. Of course we've done the usual things, but somehow there seems to be something lacking," rattled on the lady. "Maybe we need a few more convivial souls to stir things up. Perhaps we're waiting for some one, real good and lively, to appear upon the scene. Does the description chance to fit you, Mr. Bennett?" Archly.

"I think not," said gloomy Bob.

"Well, that isn't what Mrs. Ralston says about you, anyway," observed the commodore's spouse.

"What does she say?"

"'When Bob Bennett's around, things begin to hum.' So you see you have a reputation to live up to."

"I dare say. No doubt I'll live up to it, all right."

"It's really up to you to stir things up."

"I've begun." Ominously.

"Have you? How lovely!"

This didn't require an answer, for it wasn't really a question. A white ball went by them, a very pretty snoop, and pretty soon another lady and a caddy loomed on their range of vision. The lady was thin and spirituelle and she walked by with a stride. You would have said she had taken lessons of a man. She looked neither to the right nor the left. At the moment, she, at any rate, was not sociably inclined. That walk meant business. She wasn't one of those fussy beginners like the lady Bob was talking with.

"Isn't that Mrs. Clarence Van Duzen?" asked Bob.

"Yes. She, too, poor dear, has had to desert hubby. Exactions of business! Clarence simply couldn't get away. You see he's director of so many things. And poor, dear old Dan! So busy! Every day at the office! So pressed with business."

"Quite so," said Bob absently. "I mean—" He stopped. He knew Dan wasn't pressed for business and Bob couldn't utter even the suspicion of an untruth now. "Didn't exactly mean that!" he mumbled.

The lady regarded him quickly. His manner was just in the least strange. But in a moment she thought no more about it.

"You didn't happen to see Dan?" she asked.

"Yes."

"At his office, I suppose?" Dan had written he hadn't even had time for his club; that it had been just work—work all the time.

"No."

"Where, then?"

"At the club and some other places." Reluctantly.

"Other places?" Lightly. Of course she hadn't really believed quite all Dan had written about that office confinement. "How dreadfully ambiguous!" With a laugh. "What other places?"

Bob began to get uneasy. "Well, we went to a cabaret or two." No especial harm about that answer.

"Of course," said the lady. "Why not?"

Bob felt relieved. He didn't want to make trouble. He was too miserable himself. He trusted that would end the talk and now regarded the neglected ball suggestively.

"And then you went to still some other places?" went on the lady in that same light, unoffended tone.

"Ye-es," Bob had to admit.

"One of those roof gardens, perhaps, where they have entertainments?" she suggested brightly.

Bob acknowledged they had gone to a roof garden. And again, and more suggestively, he eyed the little white ball. But Mrs. Dan seemed to have forgotten all about it.

"Roof gardens," she said. "I adore roof gardens. They *are* such a boon to the people. I told dear Dan to be sure not to miss them. So nice to think of him enjoying himself instead of moping away in a stuffy old office."

Bob gazed at her suspiciously. But she had such an open face! One of those faces one can't help trusting. Mrs. Dan was just the homely, plain old-fashioned type. At least, so she seemed. Anyhow, it didn't much matter so far as Bob was concerned. He had to tell the truth. He hadn't sought this conversation. It was forced on him. He was only going the "even tenor of his way." He was, however, rather pleased that Mrs. Dan did seem in some respects different from others of her sex. Bob didn't, of course, really know much about the sex.

"So you went to the roof garden—just you and Dan," purred Mrs. Dan.

Bob didn't answer. He hoped she hadn't really put that as a question.

"Or *were* you and Dan alone?" She made it a question now.

"No-a."

"Who else were along?"

"Dickie—"

"And—?"

"Clarence."

She gazed toward Mrs. Clarence, while a shade of anxiety appeared on Bob's face. In the distance Mrs. Clarence had paused to contemplate the result of an unusually satisfactory display of skill. Mrs. Dan next glanced sidewise at her caddy, but that young man seemed to have relapsed into a condition of innocuous vacancy. He looked capable of falling asleep standing. Certainly he wasn't trying to overhear.

"Just you four men!" Mrs. Dan resumed her purring. "Or were you all alone? No ladies along?"

While expecting, of course, the negative direct, she was studying Bob and gleaning what she could, surreptitiously, or by inference. He had an eloquent face which might tell her something his lips refused to reveal. His answer almost took her breath away.

"Ye-es."

He was sorry, but he had to say it. No way out of it! Mrs. Dan's jaw fell. What she might have said can only be conjectured, for at this moment, luckily for Bob, there came an interruption.

"Tête-à-têting, instead of teeing!" broke in a jocular voice. The speaker wore ecclesiastical garments; his imposing calves were encased in episcopal gaiters. Mrs. Ralston always liked to dignify her house-parties with a religious touch, and this particular bishop was very popular with her. Bob inwardly blessed the good man for his opportune appearance. He was a ponderous wag.

"Forgive interruption," he went on, just as if Mrs. Dan who was non-amatory had been engaged in a furious flirtation. "I'll be hurrying on."

"Do," said Mrs. Dan, matching his tone, and concealing any inward exasperation that she might have felt.

"It's I who will be hurrying on," interposed Bob quickly. "You see, I'm expected to arrive at the house," he laughed.

"Looked as if you were having an interesting conversation," persisted the bishop waggishly.

"And so we were," assented Mrs. Dan. She could have stamped with vexation, but instead, she forced a smile. The dear tiresome bishop had to be borne.

"Confess you find me de trop?" he went on, shaking a finger at Bob.

"On the contrary," said Bob.

"Has to say that," laughed the good man. He did love to poke fun (or what he conceived "fun") at "fair, fat and forty." "I suppose you were positively dee-lighted to be interrupted?"

"I was," returned Bob truthfully.

"Ha! ha!" laughed the bishop.

Bob looked at him. The bishop thought he was joking, just as the hackman had. Of course, no one could say such a thing as that seriously and in the presence of the lady herself. People always didn't believe truth when they heard it. They thought telling the truth a form of crude humor, and a spark of hope-a very small one—shot through Bob's brain. Perhaps they would continue to look upon him in the light of a joker. He would be the little joker in the pack of cards and he might yet pull off that "three weeks" without pulling down the house. Only—would Miss Gerald look upon him as a joker? Intuition promptly told him she would not. His thoughts reverted to that last meeting. Think of having told her he didn't want—His offense grew more awful unto himself every moment. He ceased to remember Mrs. Dan, and saying something, he hardly knew what, Bob walked on.

Miss Gwendoline Gerald was on the big veranda when he reached the house. He would have thanked her humbly and with immense contrition for having transferred his bag and clubs hither, but as he went by, that gracious, stately young lady seemed not to see him. It was as if he had suddenly become invisible. Her face didn't even change; the proud contour expressed neither contempt nor disdain; the perfectly formed lips didn't take a more pronounced curve or grow hard.

Bob felt himself shrink. He was like that man in the story book who becomes invisible at times. The fiction man, however, attained this convenient consummation through his own volition. Bob didn't. She was the magician and he wasn't even a joker.

He managed to reach the front door without stumbling. A wild desire to attract her attention by asking her if his luggage *had* arrived safely, he dismissed quickly. It wouldn't do at all. It might imply a fear she had dumped it out, en route. And if she hadn't, such an inquiry would only emphasize the fact that she had acted as expressman—or woman—and for him!

He would go to his room at once, he told the footman. He didn't mind a few moments' solitude. If so much could happen before his house-party had begun—before he even got into the house—what might he not expect later? In one of the upper halls he encountered the man with the monocle.

"I say!" said this person. "What a jolly coincidence!"

"Think so?" said Bob. He didn't find anything "jolly" about it. On another occasion, he might have noticed that the eye behind the "window-pane" was rather twinkling, but his perceptions were not particularly keen at the present time.

In the room to which he had been assigned, Bob cast off a few garments. Then he stopped with his shirt partly off. He wondered how Miss Gerald would look the next time he saw her? Like a frozen Hebe, perhaps! Bob removed the shirt and cast it viciously somewhere. Then he selected another shirt—the first that came along, for why should he exercise care to select? It matters little what an invisible man wears. *She* wouldn't see the extra stripe or the bigger dot. Stripes couldn't rescue him from insubstantiability. Colors, too, would make no difference. Pea-green, yellow, or lavender—it was all one. Any old shirt would do. And any old tie!

When he had finished dressing, he didn't find any further excuse for remaining in his room. He couldn't consult his desires as to that. He wasn't asked there to be a hermit. He couldn't imitate Timon of Athens, Diogenes or any other of those wise old fellows who did the glorious solitude act. Diogenes told the truth, mostly, but he could live in a tub. He didn't have to participate in house-parties. Whoever invented house-parties, anyhow? They were such uncomfortable "social functions" they must have been invented by the English. Why do people want to get together? Bob could sympathize with Diogenes. Also, he could envy Timon his howling wilderness! But personally he couldn't even be a Robinson Crusoe. Would there were no other company than clawless crabs and a goat and a parrot! He would not be afraid to tell *them* the truth.

He had to go down and he did. Nemesis lurked for him below. Had Bob realized what was going to happen he would have skipped back to his room. But, as it was, he assumed a bold front. He even said to himself, "Cheer up; the worst is yet to come." It was.

CHAPTER V—TRIVIALITIES

Luncheon came and went, but nothing actually tragic happened at it. Bob didn't make more than a dozen remarks that failed to add to his popularity. He tried to be agreeable, because that was his nature. That "even-tenor-of-his-way" condition made it incumbent on him—yes, made it his sacred duty to be bright and amiable. So it was "Hence, loathed Melancholy!" and a brave endeavor to be as jocund as the poet's lines! Only those little unfortunate moments— airy preludes to larger misfortunes—had to occur, and just when he would flatter himself he was not doing so badly.

For example, when Mrs. Augustus Ossenreich Vanderpool said: "Don't you adore dogs, Mr. Bennett?"

"No. I like them." It became necessary to qualify that. "That is—not the little kind."

The lady stiffened. Her beribboned and perfumed five-thousand-dollar toy-dogs were the idolized darlings of her heart. The children might be relegated to the nursery but the canines had the run of the boudoir. They rode with her when she went out in state while the French *bonne* took the children for an airing. "And why are the 'little kind' excluded from the realm of your approbation?" observed Mrs. Vanderpool coldly.

It was quite a contract to answer that. Bob wanted to be truthful; not to say too much or too little; only just as much as he was in honor bound to say. "I think people make too much fuss over them," he answered at last. That reply seemed quite adequate and he trusted the lady would change the subject. But people had a way of not doing what he wanted them to, lately.

"What do you call 'too much fuss'?" pursued the lady persistently.

Bob explained as best he could. It was rather a thankless task and he floundered a good deal as he went about it. He wasn't going to be a bit more disagreeable than he could help, only he couldn't help being as disagreeable as he had to be. The fact that Miss Gwendoline Gerald's starry eyes were on him with cold curiosity did not improve the lucidity of his explanation. In the midst of it, she to whom he was talking, seemed somehow to detach herself from him, gradually, not pointedly, for he hardly knew just when or how she got away. She seemed just to float off and to attach herself somewhere else—to the bishop or to a certain judge Mrs. Ralston always asked to her house-parties that they might have a judicial as well as an ecclesiastical touch—and Bob's explanation died on the thin air. He let it die. He didn't have to speak truth to vacancy.

Then he tangoed, but not with Miss Gwendoline Gerald. He positively dared not approach that young lady. He didn't tango because he wanted to, but because some one set a big music-box going and he knew he was expected to tango. He did it beautifully and the young lady was charmed. She was a little dark thing, of the clinging variety, and Dickie had gone with her some. Her father owned properties that would go well with Dickie's—there'd been some talk of consolidation, but it had never come off. Papa was inclined to be stand-offish. Then Dickie began to get attentive to the little dark thing, though nothing had yet come of that either. Bob didn't own any properties but the little dark thing didn't mind that. At tangoing, he was a dream. Properties can't tango.

"You do it so well," said the little dark thing breathlessly.

"Do I?" murmured Bob, thinking of a stately young goddess, now tangoing with another fellow.

"Don't you adore it?" went on the little dark thing, nestling as close as was conventional and proper.

"I might," observed Bob. That was almost as bad as the dog question. He trusted the matter would end there.

She giggled happily. "Maybe you disapprove of modern dancing, Mr. Bennett?"

"That depends," said Bob gloomily. He meant it depended upon who was "doing the modern" with the object of your fondest affections. If you yourself were engaged in the arduous pastime with said object, you would, naturally harbor no particular objections against said modern tendencies, but if you weren't?—

Bob tangoed more swiftly. His thoughts were so bitter he wanted to run away from them. The irony of gliding rhythmically and poetically in seeming joyous abandon of movement when his heart weighed a ton! If that heaviness of heart were communicated to his legs, they would in reality be as heavy as those of a deep-sea diver, weighted down for a ten-fathom plunge.

And in thus trying to run away from his thoughts Bob whirled the little dark thing quite madly. He couldn't dance ungracefully if he tried and the little dark thing had a soul for rhythm. It was as if he were trying to run away with her. He fairly took away her breath. She was a panting little dark thing on his broad breast now, but she didn't ask him to stop. The music-box ceased to be musical and that brought them to a stop. The eyes of the little dark thing—her name was Dolly—sparkled, and she gazed up at Bob with the respect one of her tender and impressionable years has for a masculine whirlwind.

"You quite sweep one off one's feet, Mr. Bennett," she managed to ejaculate.

At that moment Miss Gwendoline passed, a divine bud glowing on either proud cheek. She caught the remark and looked at the maker of it. She noted the sparkle in the eyes. The little dark thing was a wonder with the men. She seemed to possess the knack—only second to Miss Gwendoline, in that line—of converting them into "trailers." Miss Gwendoline, though, never tried to attain this result. Men became her trailers without any effort on her part, while the little dark thing had to exert herself, but it was agreeable work. She made Bob a trailer now, temporarily. Miss Gwendoline turned her head slightly, with a gleam of surprise to watch him trail. She had noticed that Bob had danced with irresistible and almost pagan abandon. That argued enjoyment.

The little dark thing would "come in" ultimately for hundreds of belching chimneys and glowing furnaces and noisy factories—quite a snug if cacophonous legacy!—and Miss Gwendoline had only that day heard rumors that Bob's governor had fallen down and hurt himself on the "street." She, Miss Gwendoline, had not attached much importance to those rumors. People were always having little mishaps in the "street," and then bobbing up richer than ever.

But now that rumor recurred to her more vividly in the light of Bob's trailing performance and the mad abandon of his tangoing. Of course, all men are gamblers, or fortune-hunters, or something equally reprehensible, at heart! Tendency of a cynical, selfish and money-grabbing age! Miss Gwendoline was no moralist but she had lived in a wise set, where people keep their eyes open and weigh things for just what they are. Naturally a young man whose governor has gone on the rocks (though only temporarily, perhaps), might think that belching chimneys, though somewhat splotchy on the horizon and unpicturesque to the eye, might be acceptable, in a first-aid-to-the-injured sense. But Bob as a plain, ordinary fortune-hunter?— Somehow the role did not fit him.

Besides, a fortune-hunter would not bruskly and unceremoniously have refused *her* invitation to ride in the trap. And at the recollection of that affront, Miss Gwendoline's violet eyes again gleamed, until for sparkles they out-matched those of the little dark thing. However, she held herself too high to be really resentful. It was impossible she should resent anything so incomprehensible, she told herself. That would lend dignity to the offense. Therefore she could only be mildly amused by it. This was, no doubt, a properly lofty attitude, but was it a genuine one? Was she not actually at heart, deeply resentful and dreadfully offended? Pride being one of her marked characteristics, she demanded a great deal and would not accept a little.

The sparkles died from the hard violet eyes. A more tentative expression replaced that other look as her glance now passed meditatively over the dark little thing. The latter had certainly a piquant bizarre attraction. She looked as if she could be very intense, though she was of that clinging-vine variety of young woman. She wore one of those tango gowns which was odd, outre and a bit daring. It went with her personality. At the same time her innocent expression seemed a mute, almost pathetic little appeal to you *not* to think it too daring.

As Miss Gerald studied the young lady, albeit without seeming to do so and holding her own in a sprightly tango kind of talk, another thought flashed into her mind. Bob might be genuinely and sentimentally smitten. Why not? Men frequently fell in love with the little dark thing, and afterward some of them said she had a "good deal of temperament." Bob might be on a temperament-investigating quest. At any rate, it was all one to Miss Gerald. Life was a comedy. *N'est-ce-pas?* What was it Balzac called it? *La Comedie Humaine.*

Meanwhile, other eyes than Miss Gerald's were bent upon luckless Bob. Mrs. Dan and Mrs. Clarence looked as if they would like to have a word with him. Mrs. Dan even maneuvered in his direction at the conclusion of the dance while Bob watched her with ill-concealed apprehension. He detected, also, an uncanny interest in Mrs. Clarence's eyes as that masterful lady eyed him and Mrs. Dan from a distance. Mrs. Dan almost got him when—the saints be praised!—Mrs. Ralston, herself, tripped blithely up and annexed him. For the moment he was safe, but only for the moment.

A reckless desire to end it all surged through Bob's inmost being. If only his hostess would say something demanding an answer that would incur such disapprobation on her part, he would feel impelled, in the natural order of events, to hasten his departure. Maybe then (and he thrilled at the thought), she might even intimate in her chilliest manner that his *immediate* departure would be the logical sequence of some truthful spasm she, herself, had forced from him? He couldn't talk French to Mrs. Ralston now; he was in honor bound not to. He would have to speak right up in the King's English—or Uncle Sam's American.

Of course, such a consummation—Bob's being practically *forced* to take his departure—was extremely unpleasant and awful to contemplate, yet worse things could happen than that—a whole string of them, one right after another!

However, he had no such luck as to be ordered forthwith off the premises. He didn't offend Mrs. Ralston at all. That lady was very nice to him (or otherwise, from Bob's present view-point) and did most of the talking herself. Perhaps she considered that compliment (?) Bob had bestowed upon her at the Waldorf sufficient to excuse him for a while from further undue efforts at flattery. At any rate, she didn't seem to take it amiss that Bob didn't say a lot more of equally nice things in that Chesterfieldian manner and with such a perfect French accent.

But he "got in bad" that afternoon with divers and sundry other guests of Mrs. Ralston. Mrs. Augustus O. Vanderpool and Miss Gerald weren't the only ones who threw cold glances his way, for the faux pas he made—that he *had* to make—were something dreadful. For example, when some one asked him what he thought of Miss Schermerhorn's voice, he had to say huskily what was in his mind:

"It is rather too strident, isn't it?" No sugar-coating the truth! If he had said anything else he would have been compromising with veracity; he would not have spoken the thought born in his brain at the question. Of course, some one repeated what he said to Miss Schermerhorn, who came from one of the oldest families, was tall and angular, and cherished fond illusions, or delusions, that she was an amateur nightingale. The some one who repeated, had to repeat, because Miss Schermerhorn was her dearest friend and confidante. Then Miss Schermerhorn came right up to Bob and asked him if he had said it and he was obliged to answer that he had. What she said, or thought, need not be repeated. She left poor Bob feeling about as big as a caterpillar.

"How very tactful of Mr. Bennett!" was all Miss Gerald said, when Miss Dolly related to her the little incident.

"That's just what I adore in him!" gushed the temperamental little thing. "He doesn't seem to be afraid of saying anything to anybody. He's so delightfully frank!"

"Frank, certainly!" answered Miss Gerald icily.

"Anyhow, he's a regular tango-king!" murmured Miss Dolly dreamily.

"I'm so glad *you* approve of him, dear!" said Miss Gerald with an enigmatic smile. Perhaps she implied the temperamental little thing found herself in a class, all by herself, in this regard.

The latter flew over to Bob. If he was so "frank" and ingenuous about Miss Schermerhorn, perhaps he would be equally so with other persons. Miss Dolly asked him if he didn't think the bishop's sermons "just too dear?" Bob did not. "Why not?" she persisted. Bob had just been reading *The Outside of the Pot.* "Why not?" repeated Miss Dolly.

"Antediluvian!" groaned Bob, then turned a fiery red. The bishop, standing on the other side of the doorway, had overheard. Maybe Miss Dolly had known he stood there for she now giggled and fled. Bob wanted to sink through the floor, but he couldn't.

"So, sir, you think my sermons antediluvian?" said the bishop, with a twinkle of the eye. *He* never got mad, he was the best old man that way that ever happened.

"Yes, sir," replied Bob, by rote.

"Thank you," said the bishop, and rubbed his nose. Then he eyed Bob curiously. "Maybe you're right," he said. That made Bob feel awful, but he couldn't retract. The truth as he saw it!—He felt as if he were chained to the wheel of fate—the truth as he saw it, though the heavens fell!

"Of course, that's only my poor insignificant opinion," he murmured miserably.

"Every man's opinion is entitled to respect," said the bishop.

"Yes, sir," replied Bob, more miserably still.

The bishop continued to study him. "You interest me, Mr. Bennett."

"Do I?" said Bob. "I'm rather interesting to myself just now."

"You evidently agree with the author of *The Outside of the Pot*?"

"That's it." Weakly.

"Well, cheer up," said the bishop, and walked away.

Later in the day the judge might have been heard to say to the bishop that "that young Bennett cub is a good-for-nothing jackanapes"— from which it might be inferred Bob had somehow managed to rub the judge's ermine the wrong way.

"Ha! ha!" laughed the bishop. "Did some one ask him what he thought of judges?"

But the judge did not laugh. His frown was awful.

"Or was it about the 'recall'? Or the relation of judges and corporations?"

The judge looked stern as Jove. "Ass!" he muttered.

"Maybe he's a progressive," returned the bishop. "The world seems to be changing. Ought we to change with it, I wonder?"

"I don't," snapped the judge. "If the world to-day is producing such fatuous blockheads, give me the world as it was."

"The trouble is," said the bishop, again rubbing his nose, "can we get it back? Hasn't it left us behind and are we ever going to catch up?"

"Fudge!" said the judge. He and the bishop were such old friends, he could take that liberty.

Another of the sterner sex—one of Mrs. Ralston's guests—looked as if he, too, could have said: "Fudge!" His lips fairly curled when he regarded Bob. He specialized as a vivisectionist, and he was a great authority. Now Bob loved the "under-dog" and was naturally kind and sympathetic. He had been blessed—or cursed—with a very tender heart for such a compact, well-put-up, six foot or so compound of hard-headed masculinity. Miss Dolly—imp of mischief—again rather forced the talk. It must be wonderful to cut things up and juggle with hind legs and kidneys and brains and mix them all up with different animals, until a poor little cat didn't know if it had a dog's brain or its own? And was it true that sometimes the dogs me-owed, and when a cat started to purr did it wag its tail instead? This was all right from Miss Dolly, but when the conversation expanded and Bob was appealed to, it was different. "Wouldn't *you* just love to mix up the different 'parts'?" asked Miss Dolly, and put a rabbit's leg on a pussy, just to watch its expression of surprise when it started to run and found itself only able to jump, or half-jump? That got honest Bob—who couldn't have carved up a poor dumb beast, to save his life—fairly involved, and before he had staggered from that conversational morass, he had offended Authority about two dozen times. Indeed, Authority openly turned its back on him. Authority found Bob impossible.

These are fair samples of a few of his experiences. And all the while he had an uneasy presentiment that Mrs. Dan and Mrs. Clarence were waiting to get him and have *their* innings. Now, Mrs. Dan would bestow upon him a too sweet smile between games of tennis; then Mrs. Clarence would drift casually in his direction, but something would happen that would prevent a heart-to-heart duologue, and she would as casually drift away again. These hit-and-miss tactics, however, gradually got on Bob's nerves, and in consequence, he who was usually a star and a cracker jack at the game, played abominable tennis that afternoon—thus enhancing his unpopularity with divers partners who simply couldn't understand why he had fallen off so. Indeed, about every one he came in contact with was profoundly dissatisfied or disgusted with Bob. Miss Gerald, who usually played with him, now firmly but unostentatiously, avoided him, and though Bob couldn't blame her, of course, still the fact did not tend to mitigate his melancholy.

How different in the past!—that glorious, never-to-be-forgotten past! Then he had inwardly reveled and rejoiced in her lithe movements—for with all her stateliness and proud carriage, she was like a young panther for grace. Now as luckless Bob played with some one else, a tantalizing college ditty floated through his brain: "I wonder who's kissing her now?"

Of course, no one was. She wasn't that kind. Though some one, some day, would! It was in the natural order of things bound to occur, and Bob, in fancy, saw those disdainful red lips, with some one hovering over, as he swung at a white ball and sent it—well, not where he should have.

"You are playing very badly, partner," a reproving voice reminded him.

Bob muttered something. Confound that frivolous haunting song! He would dismiss the dire and absurd possibility. Some one else was with her, though, and that was sufficiently poignant. There were several of the fellows tremendously smitten in that quarter. Fine, husky athletic chaps, too! Some of them quite expert at wooing, no doubt, for devotees of house-parties become educated and acquire finesse. They don't have to tell the truth all the time, but on the contrary, are privileged to prevaricate in the most artistic manner. They can gaze into beautiful eyes and swear that they have "never before," and so on. They can perform prodigies of prevarication and "get away" with them. Bob played now even worse than before.

The sun got low at last, however, and wearily he retired to his room, to change his garments for dinner. Incidentally, he surveyed himself in the mirror with haunting earnestness of gaze. Had he grown perceptibly older? He thought he could detect a few lines of care on his erstwhile unsullied brow, and with a sigh, he turned away to array himself in the customary black—or "glad rags"—which seemed now, however, but the habiliments of woe. Then he descended to receive a new shock; he found out that Mrs. Ralston had assigned Mrs. Dan to him, to take in to dinner. Drearily Bob wondered if it were mere chance that he had drawn Mrs. Dan for a dinner prize, or if Mrs. Dan herself had somehow brought about that, to her, desired consummation. As he gave Mrs. Dan his arm he saw

Mrs. Clarence exchange glances with the commodore's good lady. Mrs. Ralston went in with the monocle man.

CHAPTER VI—DINNER

Mrs. Dan dallied with Bob, displaying all the artifices of an old campaigner. Of course, she had no idea how easy it might be for her to learn all she wanted to. She could not know he was like a barrel or puncheon of information and that all she had to do was to pull the plug and let information flow out. She regarded Bob more in the light of a safety vault; the bishop's interruption had put him on his guard and she would have to get through those massive outer-doors of his reserve, before she could force the many smaller doors to various boxes full of startling facts.

It was a fine tableful of people, of which they were a part. Wealth, beauty, brains and brawn were all there. An orchestra played somewhere. Being paid performers you didn't see them and as distance lends enchantment to music, on most occasions, the result was admirable. Delicate orchids everywhere charmed with their hues without exuding that too obtrusive perfume of commoner flowers. Mrs. Ralston was an orchid enthusiast and down on the Amazon she kept an orchid-hunter who, whenever he found a new variety, sent her a cable.

So Mrs. Dan started on orchids with Bob. She hadn't the slightest interest in orchids, but she displayed a simulated interest that sounded almost like real interest. Mrs. Dan hadn't practised on society, or had society practise on her, all these years for nothing. She could get that simulated-interested tone going without any effort. But Bob's attention wandered, and he gazed toward Miss Gerald who occupied a place quite a distance from him.

Mrs. Dan, failing to interest Bob on orchids, now took another tack. She sailed a conversational course on caviar. Men usually like things to eat, and to talk about them, especially such caviar as this. But Bob eyed the almost priceless Malasol as if it were composed of plain, ordinary fish-eggs. He didn't even enthuse when he took a sip of Moselle that matched the Malasol and had more "bouquet" than the flowers. So Mrs. Dan, again altering her conversational course, sailed merrily before the wind amid the breeze of general topics and gay light persiflage. She was at her best now. There wasn't anything she didn't know something about. She talked plays, operas and amusements which gradually led her up to roof gardens. She took her time, though, before laying the bowsprit of her desires straight in the real direction she wished to go. She knew she could proceed cautiously and circumspectly, that there was no need for hurry; the meal would be fairly prolonged. Mrs. Ralston's dinners were elaborate affairs; there might even be a few professional entertainment features between courses.

"And speaking about roof gardens," went on Mrs. Dan, looking any way save at Bob, "I believe you were telling me, only this afternoon, how you and dear Dan were finally driven to them as a last resort. Poor Dan! So glad to hear he could get a breath of fresh air in that stuffy old town! Just hated to think of him confined to some stuffy old office. Men work too hard in our strenuous, bustling country, don't you think so? And then they break down prematurely. I've always told Dan," she rattled on, "to enjoy himself—innocently, of course." She paused to take breath. "Don't you think men work too hard in America, Mr. Bennett?" she repeated.

"Sometimes," said Bob.

She gave him a quick look. Perhaps she was proceeding rather fast, though Bob didn't look on his guard. "As I told you, I adore roof gardens. But you were telling me you men were not alone. What harm!" she gurgled. "Some people," talking fast, "are so prudish. I'm sure we're not put in the world to be that. Don't you agree?"

"Of course," said Bob absently. He didn't like the way that fellow down on the other side of the table was gazing into Miss Gwendoline's eyes. "I beg your pardon. I—I don't think I caught that."

"We were saying there were some wom—ladies with you," said Mrs. Dan quickly. Too quickly! She strove to curb her precipitancy. "You remember? You told me?" Her voice trailed off, as if it were a matter of little interest.

"Did I?" Bob caught himself up with a jerk. He felt now as if he were a big fish being angled for, and gazed at her with sudden apprehension. The lady's, mien however, was reassuring.

"Of course," she laughed. "Don't you remember?"

"I believe I did say something of the kind." Slowly. He had had to.

"Surely you don't deny now?" she continued playfully.

"No." He had not spared himself. He couldn't spare Dan. The lady's manner seemed to say: "*I* don't care a little bit." Anyhow, the evening in question had passed innocently, if frivolously, enough. No harm would come to Dan in consequence. And again Bob's interest floated elsewhere.

He noticed Miss Gwendoline did not seem exactly averse to letting that fellow by her side gaze into her eyes. Confound the fellow! He had one of those open honest faces. A likable chap, too! One of the Olympian-game brand! A weight-putter, or hammer-thrower, or something of the kind. Bob could have heaved considerable of a sledge himself at that moment.

"Of course, boys will be boys," prattled Mrs. Dan at his side, just in the least stridently. "I suppose you sat down and they just happened along and sat down, too! You couldn't very well refuse to let them, could you? That wouldn't have been very polite?" She hardly knew what she was saying herself now. Though a conversational general, on most occasions, her inward emotion was now running apace. It was almost beating her judgment in the race. She tried to pull herself together. "Why, in Paris, doing the sights at the Jardin or the Moulin Rouge, or the Casino de Paris, every one takes it or them—these chance acquaintances—as a matter of course. *Pour passer le temps!* And why not?" With a shrug and in her sprightliest manner. "So the ladies in this instance, as you were saying, came right up, too, and—?"

She paused. That was crude—clumsy—even though she rattled it off as if without thinking. She was losing all her finesse. But again, to her surprise, the fish took the bait. She did not know Bob's predicament—that *he* couldn't finesse.

"Yes, they came up," said Bob reluctantly, though pleased that Mrs. Dan appeared such a good kind of fellow.

"Show-girls?" asked the lady quickly.

"Well—ah!—two of them were."

"Two? And what were the others?"

Bob again regarded the lady apprehensively, but her expression was eminently reassuring. It went with the music, the bright flowers and the rest of the gay scene. Mrs. Dan's smile was one of unadulterated enjoyment; she didn't seem displeased at all. Must be she wasn't displeased! Perhaps she was like some of those model French wives who aren't averse at all to having other ladies attentive to their husbands? Mrs. Dan had lived in Paris and might have acquired with a real accent an accompanying broad-mindedness of character. That might be what made the dear old commodore act so happy most of the time, and so juvenile, too! Mrs. Dan *looked* broad-minded. She had a broad face and her figure was broad—very! At the moment she seemed fairly to radiate broad-mindedness and again Bob felt glad—on the commodore's account. He had nothing to feel glad about, himself, with that confounded hammer-thrower—

"Who were the others, did you say?" repeated Mrs. Dan, in her most broad-minded tone.

She seemed only talking to make conversation and looked away unconcernedly as she spoke. Lucky for Dan she was broad-minded—that they had once been expatriates together! Even if she hadn't been, however, Bob would have had to tell the truth.

"Who were the others?" he repeated absently, one eye on Miss Gerald. "Oh, they were 'ponies.'"

"'Ponies,'" said the lady giving a slight start and then recovering. "I beg your pardon, but—ah—do you happen to be referring to the horse-show?"

"Not at all," answered Bob. "The ponies I refer to," wearily, "are not equine." These technical explanations were tiresome. At that moment he was more concerned with the hammer-thrower, who had evidently just hurled a witticism at Miss Gerald, for both were laughing. Would that Bob could have caught the silvery sound of her voice! Would he had been near enough! Across the table, the little dark thing threw him a few consolatory glances. He had almost forgotten about her. Miss Dolly's temperamental eyes seemed to say "Drink to me only with thine eyes," and Bob responded recklessly to the invitation. The little dark thing seemed the only one on earth who was good to him. He drank to her with his eyes—without becoming intoxicated. Then she held a glass to her lips and gazed at him over it. He held one to his and did likewise. He should have become doubly intoxicated, but he didn't. He set down his glass mournfully. Miss Gerald noticed this sentimental little byplay, but what Bob did was, of course, of no moment to her.

"Ponies, Mr. Bennett? And not equine?" Mrs. Dan with difficulty succeeded in again riveting Bob's wandering attention. "Ah, of course!" Her accents rising frivolously. "How stupid of me!" Gaily. "You mean the kind that do the dancing in the musical shows." And Mrs. Dan glanced a little furtively at her right.

But on that side the good bishop was still expounding earnestly to the lady he had brought in. He was not in the least interested in what Mrs. Dan and Bob were saying. He was too much concerned in what he was saying himself. At Bob's left sat the young lady who had been his partner at tennis in the afternoon but she, obviously, took absolutely no interest in Bob now. He had a vague recollection of having been forced to say something in her hearing, earlier in the day, that had sounded almost as bad as his tennis-playing had been. Truth, according to the philosophers, is beautiful. Only it doesn't seem to be! This young lady had turned as much of the back of a bare "cold shoulder" on Bob at the table as she could. In fact, she made it quite clear Mrs. Dan could have the young man entirely to herself. So Mrs. Dan and Bob were really as alone, for confidential conversational purposes, as if they had been secluded in some retired cozy-corner.

"Two show-girls and two ponies!" Mrs. Dan went on blithely. "That made one apiece." With a laugh. "Who got the ponies?"

"Clarence got one."

"And Dan?"

Bob nodded. He had to, it was in the contract. The lady laughed again right gaily.

"Dan always did like the turf," she breathed softly. "So fond of the track, or anything equine."

For the moment Bob became again almost suspicious of her, she was *such* a "good fellow"! And Bob wasn't revengeful; because he had suffered himself he didn't wish the commodore any harm. Of course it would be rather a ghastly joke on the commodore if Mrs. Dan wasn't such a "good fellow" as she seemed. But Bob dismissed that contingency. He was helpless, anyway. He was no more than a chip in a stream. The current of Mrs. Dan's questions carried him along.

"And what did the pony Dan got, look like?"

"I think she had reddish hair."

"How lurid! I suppose you all had a few ponies with the ponies?" Jocularly.

"Yes," said the answering-machine.

"I suppose the ponies had names? They usually do," she rattled on.

"Yes. They had names, of course."

"What was Dan's called?"

The orchestra was playing a little louder now—one of those wild pieces—a rhapsody!

"Don't know her real name."

"Her stage name, then?"

"Not sure of that!" Doubtfully.

"But Dan *must* have called her something?" With a gay little laugh.

"Yes." Bob hesitated. In spite of that funereal feeling, he couldn't suppress a grin. "He called her Gee-gee."

"Gee-gee!" almost shrieked the lady. Then she laughed harder than ever. She was certainly a good actress. At that moment she caught Mrs. Clarence Van Duzen's eye; it was coldly questioning.

"And what did the pony Clarence got, look like?" Mrs. Dan had passed the stage of analyzing or reasoning clearly. She didn't even ask herself why Bob wasn't more evasive. She didn't want to know whether it was that "good-fellow" manner on her part that had really deceived him into unbosoming the truth to her, or whether—well, he had been drinking too much? He held himself soberly enough, it is true, but there are strong men who look sober and can walk a chalk line, when they aren't sober at all. Bob might belong to that class. She thought she had detected something on his breath when he passed on the links and he might have been "hitting it up" pretty hard since, on the side, with some of the men. In "vino veritas"! But whether "vino," or denseness on his part, she was sure of the "veritas." Instinct told her she had heard the truth.

"And Clarence's pony—did she have red hair, too?" She put the question in a different way, for Bob was hesitating again.

"No."

"What was its hue?"

"Peroxide, I guess." Gloomily.

"Is that all you remember?" Mrs. Dan now was plying questions recklessly, regardlessly, as if Bob were on the witness-stand and she were state prosecutor.

"About all. Oh!—her nose turned up and she had a freckle."

"How interesting!" Mrs. Dan's laugh was rather forced, and she and Mrs. Clarence again exchanged glances, but Bob didn't notice. "And what was she called?" Breathing a little hard.

"Gid-up," said Bob gravely.

"'Gid-up'!" Again the lady almost had a paroxysm, but whether or not of mirth, who shall say. "Gee-gee and Gid-up!" Her broad bosom rose and fell.

"Telegram, sir!" At that moment Bob heard another voice at his elbow. Across the table the man with the monocle was gazing at him curiously.

CHAPTER VII—VARYING VICISSITUDES

A footman had brought the message, which Bob now took and opened mechanically. It was from the commodore.

"For heaven's sake," it ran, "return at once to New York Will explain."

Bob eyed it gloomily. The commodore must have been considerably rattled when he had sent that.

"Any answer, sir?" said the footman.

Bob shook his head. What could he answer? He couldn't run away now; the commodore ought to know that. Of all fool telegrams!—

"A business message, I suppose?" purred the lady at his side. "I trust it is nothing very important, to call you away?"

"No, I shouldn't call it important," said Bob. "Quite unnecessary, I should call it."

He crumpled up the message and thrust it into his pocket. At that moment one of Mrs. Ralston's paid performers—a high-class monologist—began to earn his fee. He was quite funny and soon had every one laughing. Bob strove to forget his troubles and laugh too. Mrs. Dan couldn't very well talk to him now, and relieved from that lady's pertinent prattle, he gradually let that "dull-care grip" slip from his resistless fingers. Welcoming the mocking goddess of the cap and bells, he yielded to the infectious humor and before long forgot the telegram and everything save that crop of near-new stories.

But when the dinner was finally over, he found himself, again wrapped in deep gloom, wandering alone on the broad balcony. He didn't just know how he came to be out there all alone—whether he drifted away from people or whether they drifted away from him. Anyhow he wasn't burdened with any one's company. He entertained a vague recollection that several people had turned their backs on him. So if he was forced to lead a hermit's life it wasn't his fault. Probably old Diogenes hadn't *wanted* to live in that tub; people had made him. They wouldn't stand him in a house. There wasn't room for him and any one else in the biggest house ever built. So the only place where truth could find that real, cozy, homey feeling was *alone* in a tub. And things weren't any better to-day. Nice commentary on our boasted "advanced civilization!"

Bob felt as if he were the most-alone man in the world! Why, he was so lonesome, he wasn't even acquainted with himself. This was only his "double" walking here. He knew now what that German poet was driving at in those *Der Doppleganger* verses. His "double" was alone. Where was he?—the real he—the original ego? Hanged if he knew! He looked up at the moon, but it couldn't tell him. At the same time, in spite of that new impersonal relationship he had established toward himself, he felt he ought to be immensely relieved in one respect. There would be no "cozy-cornering" for him that evening. He had the whole wide world to himself. He could be a wandering Jew as well as a *Doppleganger*, if he wanted to.

He made out now two shadows, or figures, in the moonlight. Mrs. Dan and Mrs. Clarence were walking and talking together, but somehow he wasn't at all curious about them. His mental faculties seemed numbed, as if his brain were way off somewhere—between the earth and the moon, perhaps. Then he heard the purring of a car, which seemed way off, too. He saw Mrs. Dan and Mrs. Clarence get into the car and heard Mrs. Dan murmur something about the village and the telegraph office, and the car slid downward. Bob watched its rear light receding this way and that, like a will-o'-the-wisp, or a lonesome firefly, until it disappeared on the winding road. A cool breeze touched him without cooling his brow. Bob threw away a cigar. What's the use of smoking when you don't taste the weed?

He wondered what he should do now? Go to bed, or—? It was too early for bed. He wouldn't go to bed at that hour, if he kept to that even-tenor-of-his-way condition. He hadn't violated any condition, so far. Those fellows who had inveigled him into this wild and woolly moving-picture kind of an impossible freak performance would have to concede that. There could be no ground for complaint that he wasn't living up to the letter and spirit of his agreement, even at the sacrifice of his most sacred feelings. Yes, by yonder gracious lady of the glorious moon! He wondered where *his* gracious lady was now and what she was doing? Of course, the hammer-thrower was with her.

"Are you meditating on your loneliness, Mr. Bennett?" said a well-remembered voice. The tones were even and composed. They were also distantly cold. Bob wheeled. Stars of a starry night! It was she.

She came right up and spoke to him—the pariah—the abhorred of many! His heart gave a thump and he could feel its hammering as his glowing eyes met the beautiful icy ones.

"How did you get rid of him?" he breathed hoarsely.

"Him?" said Miss Gwendoline Gerald, in a tone whose stillness should have warned Bob.

"That sledge-hammer man? That weight-putter? That Olympian village blacksmith, I mean? The fellow with the open honest face?"

"I don't believe I understand," observed the young lady, straight and proud as a wonderful princess in the moonlight. Bob gazed at her in rapture. Talk about the shoulders of that girl who had given him the cold shoulder at the dinner-table!—Miss Gwendoline's shoulders were a thousand times superior; they would cause any sculptor to rave. Their plastic beauty was that of the purest marble in that pure light. And that pure, perfect face, likewise bathed in the celestial flood of light—until now, never had he quite realized what he had lost, in losing her.

"But never mind about explaining," went on the vision, apropos of Bob's Olympian, village-blacksmith remark. "I didn't come to discuss generalities."

"Of course not," assented Bob eagerly.

The music from the house now sounded suspiciously like a trot. Miss Gerald saw, though indistinctly, a face look out of the door. It might have been the little dark thing peering around for Bob, for she was quite capable of doing that. Bob didn't notice her—if it were she. He had eyes for but one. He was worshiping in that distant, eager, hungry, lost-soul kind of a way. Miss Gerald's glance returned to Bob.

"Will you be so good as to take a turn or two about the garden with me?" she said in a calm, if hard and matter-of-fact tone. A number of people were now approaching from the other end of the broad, partially-enclosed space and Miss Gerald had observed them.

"Will I?" Bob's accents expressed more eloquently than words how he felt about complying with that request. Would a man dying of thirst drink a goblet of cool, sparkling spring-water? Would a miser refuse gold? Or a canine a bone? "Will I?" repeated Bob, ecstatically, and threw back his shoulders. Thus men go forth to conquer. He did not realize how unique he was at the moment, for he was quite swept away. The girl cast on him a quick enigmatic glance, then led the way.

Sometimes his eyes turned to the stars and sometimes toward her as they moved along. In the latter instance, they were almost proprietary, as if he knew she ought to belong to him, though she never would. The stars seemed to say she was made for him, the breeze to whisper it. Of course, he hadn't really any right to act "proprietary"; it was taking a certain poetic license with the situation. Once Miss Gerald caught that proprietary look and into the still depths of her own gaze sprang an expression of wonder. But it didn't linger; her eyes became once more coldly, proudly assured.

Bob didn't ask whither she was leading him, or what fate had in store for him. Sufficient unto the present moment was the happiness thereof! A fool's paradise is better than no paradise at all. He didn't stop now to consider that he might be playing with verity when he hugged to his breast an illusory joy.

She didn't talk at first, but he didn't find anything to complain of in that. It was blissful enough just to swing along silently at her side. He didn't have to bother about the truth-proposition when she didn't say anything. He could yield to a quiet unadulterated joy in the stillness. If denied, temporarily, the music of her voice, he was, at least, privileged to visualize her, as she walked along the narrow path with the freedom and grace of a young goddess, or one of Diana's lithe forest attendants. The vision, at length, stopped at the verge of a terrace where stood an Italian-looking little summer-house, or shelter. No one was in it, and she entered. They wouldn't be disturbed here.

She leaned on a marble balustrade and for a moment looked down upon the shadowy tree-tops. The moonlight glinted a rounded white arm. Bob breathed deep. It was a spot for lovers. But there was still no love-light in Miss Gerald's eyes. They met the gaze of Bob, who hadn't yet come out of that paradoxical trance, with cold contemplation.

"Do you know what people are beginning to say about you, Mr. Bennett?" began the vision, with considerable decision in her tones.

"No," said Bob.

"Some of them are wondering—well, if you are mentally quite all right."

"Are they?" It was more the silvery sound of her voice than what people were saying that interested Bob.

"The judge and Mrs. Vanderpool have agreed that you aren't. People are a little divided in the matter."

"Indeed?" observed Bob. Of course if people were "divided," that would make it more interesting for them. Give them something to talk about!

"The doctor agrees with the judge and Mrs. Vanderpool, but the bishop seems inclined to give you the benefit of the doubt," went on Miss Gerald, her silvery tones as tranquil and cold as moonlight on the still surface of an inland sea. "He said something about inherited eccentricities, probably just beginning to crop out. Or suggested it might be—well, a pose."

"Very nice of the bishop!" muttered Bob. "Benefit of the doubt? Quite so! Fine old chap!"

"Is that all you have to say?" said Miss Gerald, a faint note of scorn in her voice now. As she spoke she leaned slightly toward him. The moonlight touched the golden hair.

"Maybe he felt he had to differ," remarked Bob, intent on the golden hair (it wasn't golden out here, of course) and the stars beyond. "He might not really differ at heart, but he had to seem broad and charitable. Ecclesiastical obligation, or habit, don't you see!"

"I don't quite see," said the girl, though her bright eyes looked capable of seeing a great deal.

"No?" murmured Bob. Some of that paradoxical happiness seemed to be fading from him. He couldn't hold it; it seemed as elusive as moonshine. If only she would stand there silently and let him continue to worship her, like that devout lover in the song—in "distant reverence." It wasn't surely quite consistent for a goddess to be so practical and matter-of-fact.

"There are others who agree with the doctor and the judge and Mrs. Vanderpool," continued the girl.

"You mean about my having a screw loose?"

"Exactly." Crisply. "And some of them have consulted me."

"And what did you say?" Quickly.

"I'm afraid I couldn't enlighten them. I believe I suggested that sun theory—although it really wasn't blistering hot to-day, and you," with inimitable irony, "look capable of standing a little sunshine."

"Yes, I feel as if I could stand a whole lot," said Bob gloomily.

"Also I said," unmindful of this last remark, "there is sometimes a method in eccentricity, or madness. Lord Stanfield agreed with me. He said he found you an 'interesting young man.'"

"Did he? Confound his impudence!" That monocle-man certainly did ruffle Bob.

"You forget he's an old friend of my aunt's." Severely. "As I was saying, Lord Stanfield found you 'interesting,' and we agreed there might be a method," studying him closely, "but when we came to search for one, we couldn't find it."

She didn't ask a question, so he didn't have to reply.

"Mr. Bennett, why did you answer me like that down in the village?"

Bob hung his head. He felt worse than a boy detected stealing apples. "Had to," he muttered desperately.

"Why?" There was no mercy in that still pitiless voice.

Bob took another long breath. "Please don't ask me," he pleaded after an ominous pause. That wasn't not telling the truth; it was only temporizing.

The violet eyes gleamed dangerously. "I'm just a little bit curious," said the girl in the same annihilating tone. "In the light of subsequent proceedings, you will understand! And as Mrs. Ralston's niece! Aunt doesn't quite realize things yet. The others have spared her feelings. I haven't, of course, gone to her. Aunt and I never 'talk over' our guests." Proudly.

That made Bob wince. He looked at her with quite helpless eyes. "Maybe she will order me off the premises before long," he said eagerly. "I have already been considering the possibility of it. Believe me," earnestly, "it would be the best way. Can't you see I'm—dangerous—positively dangerous? I'm worse than a socialist—an anarchist! Why, a Russian nihilist couldn't make half the trouble in the world that I can. I'm a regular walking disturber. Disaster follows in my path." Bitterly. "Some people look upon me as worse than the black plague. Now if your aunt would only turn me out? You see I can't go unless she does. Got to think of that even-tenor-of-my-way! But if she would only quietly intimate—or set the dog on me—"

The girl gazed at him more steadily. "I wonder if the judge and the doctor and Mrs. Vanderpool aren't right, after all?" she observed slowly. "Let me look in your eyes, Mr. Bennett." Bob did. Miss Gerald had heard that one could always tell crazy people by their eyes. She intended to sift this matter to the bottom and therefore proceeded with characteristic directness. Folk that were—well, "off," she had been told, invariably showed that they were that, by a peculiar glitter.

Miss Gerald gazed a few moments critically, steadily and with unswerving intention. Bob withstood that look with mingled wretchedness and rapture. He began to forget that they were just the eyes of a would-be expert on a mental matter, and his own eyes, looking deeper and deeper in those wonderful violet depths (he stood so she got the benefit of the moonlight) began to gleam with that old, old gleam Miss Gerald could remember in the past. Bob had never *talked* love in those blissful days of yore, but he had looked it.

"I don't see any signs of insanity," said the girl at length with cold assurance. That gleam wasn't a glitter. Nothing crazy about it! She had seen it too often in other men's eyes, as well as in Bob's—not perhaps to such a marked degree in other men's eyes,-but sufficiently so that she was fairly familiar with it. "You look normal enough to me."

"Thank you," said Bob gratefully.

"And that's just why"—a slight frown on the smooth fine brow—"I don't understand. Of course, a man not normal, might have answered as you did me (I'm not thinking of it as a personal matter, you will understand)."

"Oh, I understand that," returned Bob. "I'm just a problem, not a person." She made him quite realize that. She made it perfectly and unmistakably apparent that he was, unto her, as some example in trigonometry, or geometry, or algebra, and she wanted to find the "solution." He was an "X"—the unknown quantity. The expression on her patrician features was entirely scholastic and calculating. Bob now felt the ardor of his gaze becoming cold as moonlight. This wasn't a lovers' bower; it was only a *palestra*, or an observatory.

"You haven't answered me yet," she said.

No diverting her from her purpose! She was certainly persistent.

"You insist I shall tell you why I didn't want to see you?"

She looked at him quickly. "That isn't what I asked, Mr. Bennett. I asked you to explain that remark in the village."

"Same thing!" he murmured. "And it's rather hard to explain, but if I've got to—?" He looked at her. On her face was the look of proud unyielding insistence. "Of course, I've got to tell you the truth," said Bob, and his tone now was dead and dull. "In the first place, dad's busted, clean down and out, and—well, I thought I wouldn't see you any more."

"I fail to see the connection." Her tones were as metallic as a voice like hers could make them.

"It's like this!" said Bob, ruffling his hair. Here was a fine romantic way to make an avowal. "You see I was in love with you," he observed, looking the other way and addressing one of the furthermost stars of the heaven. "And—and—when a fellow's in love—and he can't—ah!—well, you know—ask the girl—you understand?"

"Very vaguely," said Miss Gerald. Bob's explanation, so far, was one of those explanations that didn't explain. If he had so heroically made up his mind not to see her, he could have stayed away, of course, from the Ralston house. He couldn't explain how he was bound to accept the invitation to come, on account of being in "honor bound" to that confounded commodore, et al., to do so. There were bound to be loose ends to his explanation. Besides, those other awfully unpleasant things that had happened? He had to tell the truth, but he couldn't tell why he was telling the truth. That had been the understanding.

Miss Gerald, at this point, began to display some of those alert and analytical qualities of mind that had made her father one of the great railroad men of his day. For an instant she had turned her head slightly at Bob's avowal—who shall say why? It may be she had felt the blood rush swiftly to her face, but if so a moment later she looked at him with that same icy calm. One hand had tightened on the cold balustrade, but Bob hadn't noticed that. She plied him now with a number of questions. She kept him on the gridiron and while he wriggled and twisted she stirred up the coals, displaying all the ability of an expert stoker. He was supersensitive about seeing her and yet as a free agent (she thought him that) he *had* seen her. From her point of view, his mental processes were hopelessly illogical— worse than that. Yet she knew he was possessed of a tolerable mentality and a good-enough judgment for one who had in his composition a slight touch of recklessness.

"I give it up," she said at length wearily.

"Do you? Oh, thank you!" exclaimed Bob gratefully. "And if your aunt orders me from the place—"

"But why can't you just go, if you want to? I'm sure no one will detain you." Haughtily.

"Can't explain, only it's impossible. Like Prometheus bound to the rock for vultures to peck at, unless—"

"How intelligible! And what a happy simile—under the circumstances!" with far-reaching scorn. "What if I should tell my aunt that her guest compared himself to—?"

"That's the idea!" returned Bob enthusiastically. "Tell her that! Then, by jove, she would—Promise me! Please!"

"Of course," said the girl slowly, "my diagnosis must be wrong." Or perhaps she meant that she had lost faith in that glitter-theory.

"If you only *could* understand!" burst from Bob explosively. It was nature calling out, protesting against such a weight of anguish.

But Miss Gerald did not respond. A statue could not have appeared more unaffected and unsympathetic. She had half turned as if to go; then she changed her mind and lingered. It annoyed her to feel she had been baffled, for she was a young woman who liked to drive right to the heart of things. Her father had been called a "czar" in his world, and she had inherited, with other of his traits, certain imperious qualities. So for a moment or two she stood thinking.

An automobile from the village went by them and proceeded to the house. It contained Mrs. Dan and Mrs. Clarence returning from the telegraph office, but Bob hardly saw it, or was aware who were its occupants. Miss Gerald absorbed him to the exclusion of all else now. He had no mind for other storms that might be gathering. Suddenly the girl turned on him with abrupt swiftness.

CHAPTER VIII—NEW COMPLICATIONS

"Is your father's embarrassment serious?" she asked.

Bob looked startled. He didn't like the way she had shifted the conversation. "Pretty bad," he answered.

"I believe, though, it's customary for men on the 'street' not to stay 'downed,' as they say?"

"Don't know as it's an invariable rule," returned Bob evasively. Then realizing it wouldn't do to be evasive: "As a matter of fact, I don't believe I'm very well posted as to that," he added.

"What does your father say?" she asked abruptly.

Bob would much rather not have talked about that with her. But— "Dad says there is no hope," he had to say.

Miss Gerald was silent for a moment. As a child she remembered a very gloomy period in her own father's career—when the "street" had him "cornered." She remembered the funereal atmosphere of the big old house—the depression on nearly every one's face—how everything had seemed permeated with impending tragedy. She remembered how her father looked at her, a great gloomy ghost of himself with somber burning eyes. She remembered how seared and seamed his strong and massive face had become in but a few days. But that was long ago and he had long since left her for good. The vivid impression, however, of that gloomy period during her childhood remained with her. It had always haunted her, though her father had not been "downed" in the end. He had emerged from the storm stronger than ever.

The girl shot a sidewise look at Bob, standing now with his arms folded like Hamlet. Perhaps he had come from such a funereal house as she, herself, so well remembered? Had dad's trouble, or tragedy, weighed on him unduly? Had it made him—for the moment—just slightly irresponsible? Miss Gerald, as has been intimated, had frankly liked Bob as an outdoor companion, or an indoor one, too, sometimes, for that matter. He was one of the few men, for example, she would "trot" with. He could "trot" in an eminently respectful manner, being possessed of an innate refinement, or chivalry, which certainly seemed good to her, after some of those other wild Terpsichorean performances of myriad masculine manikins in the mad world of Milliondom.

"I suppose your father has taken his trouble much to heart?" Miss Gerald now observed.

"Not a bit."

"No?" In surprise.

"No."

"Why not?"

"Said he looked to me to keep him in affluence the rest of his days."

"To you?"

"That's right."

"But how?—What are you going to do?"

"Hustle."

"At what?"

"Don't know. Got to find out."

"What did you plan doing, when at college?"

"Nothing."

"Is it"—Miss Gerald got back to where she had been before—"the sense of awful responsibility," with slight sarcasm, "that has turned your brain?"

"I'm not crazy."

"No?" She remembered that most people in asylums say that.

"Though I may be in a matter of three weeks," Bob added, more to himself than to her.

"Why three weeks?"

"Well, if I don't—just shouldn't happen to go crazy during that time, I'll be all right, after that."

"Why do you allow a specified period for your mental deterioration?"

"*I* didn't allow it."

"Who did?"

"Can't tell you."

Miss Gerald pondered on this answer. It would seem as if Bob had "hallucinations," if nothing worse. He was possessed of the idea, no doubt, that he would go crazy within three weeks. He didn't realize that the "deterioration," she referred to, might have already begun. He looked normal enough, though, had the most normal-looking eyes. Could it be that he was acting? And if he was acting, why was he? That seemed incomprehensible. Anyhow, it couldn't be a sense of responsibility that had "upset" Bob. She became sure of that now. He played a losing game with too much dash and brilliancy! Hadn't she seen him at polo—hadn't she held her breath and thrilled when he had "sailed in" and with irresistible vim snatched victory out of defeat? No; Bob wasn't a "quitter."

"So your father looks to you to support him?"

"So he said. The governor's a bit of a joker though, you know. He may be only putting up a bluff to try me out."

"What did he advise you to do?"

Bob shivered. "Matrimonial market."

"You mean—?"

"Heiress." Succinctly.

"Any particular one?"

"Dad did mention a name."

"Not—?" She looked at him.

"Yes."

An awful pause.

"Now you know why I didn't want to see you," said Bob, in that even fatalistic voice. "First place, I wouldn't ask you to marry me, if you were the last girl in the world! Second place, I was afraid if I saw you, some of these things dad said to try me, would be bound to pop out. You mustn't think badly of dad, Miss Gerald. As I've said, he didn't mean a word of it. He was only sizing me up. Don't I know that twinkle in his eye? Just wanted to see if I'm as lazy and good-for-nothing as some chaps brought up with the silver spoon. Why, he'd—honestly, dad would just kick me, if I took his advice. Why, if I went back home to-morrow," went on Bob, warming to the subject, "and told him we were engaged"—the girl moved slightly—"and were going to be married right off"—the girl moved again—"why—why, old as I am, dad would take off his coat and give me a good trouncing. That's the kind of a man dad is. I see it all now."

He really believed he did—and for the first time. He felt he had solved the mystery of dad's manner and conduct. It *had* been a mystery, but the solution had come to him like an inspiration. Dad wanted to see whether he would arise to the occasion. He had told him he didn't believe he was worth his salt just to see his backbone stiffen. He had alluded to that other way of repairing the "busted family credit" just to observe the effect on Bob. And how dad must have chuckled inwardly at Bob's response! Why, they'd almost had a scene, he and good old dad. Bob could smile at it now—if he could smile at anything. He certainly had been a numskull. Dad, pulling in fish somewhere, was probably still chuckling to himself, and wondering how Bob would work out the problem.

"Dad was always just like that when I was a boy," he confided to Miss Gerald, now standing more than ever like a marble lady in the moonlight. "He would propose the contrariest things! Always trying and testing me. Guess that's why he acted so happy when he went broke. Thought it would make a man of me! By jove, that's it! Why, he was as care-free as a boy with a new top!"

"Was he, indeed?" said Miss Gerald, studying Mr. Robert Bennett with eyes that looked very deep now, beneath the imperious brows. "How nice!" Oh, that tone was distant. It might have been wafted from one who stood on an iceberg.

"Isn't it?" Bob heaved a sigh. "I'm not afraid of you any more," he said, "now that I've got that off my chest."

Again Miss Gerald shivered slightly, but whether at the slang or not, was not apparent.

"You can't frighten me any more," said Bob.

"But why," said Miss Gerald, "did you tell me, at all, of dad's—as you call him—charming suggestion?"

"Had to. Didn't you ask me?" In faint surprise. Then he remembered she didn't know he *had* to tell the truth. That made him look rather foolish—or "imbecile," in the light of all those other proceedings. Miss Gerald's brow contracted once more. Again she might be asking herself if Master Robert was acting? Was this but gigantic, bombastic, Quixotic "posing" after all? It was too extraordinary to speak of such things as he had spoken of, to her! Did he only want to appear different? Did he seek to combine Apollo with Bernard Shaw in his attitude toward society? Or had he been reading Chesterton and was he but striving to present in his own personality a futurist's effect of upside-downness? Miss Gerald felt now the way she had at the modernists' exhibition, when she had gazed and gazed at what was apparently a load of wood falling down-stairs, and some one had told her to find the lady. It was about as difficult to-night to find the real Mr. Bennett—the happy-go-lucky Bob Bennett of last month or last week—as it had been to find that lady where appeared only chaotic kindling wood.

Miss Gerald let the cool air fan her brow for a few moments. This young man was, at least, exhilarating. She felt a little dizzy. Meanwhile Bob looked at her with that sad silly smile.

"You can't ask me any questions that will disconcert me now," he boasted.

Miss Gerald looked at him squarely. "Will you marry me?" she said.

It was a coup. Her father had been capable of just such coups as that. He would hit the enemy in the most unexpected manner in the most unexpected quarter, and thus overwhelm his foes. Miss Gerald might not mean it; she, most likely, only said it. Under the circumstances, to get at the truth herself, she was justified in saying almost anything. If he were but posing, she would prick the bubble of his pretense. If those grandiloquent, and, to her, totally unnecessary protestations didn't mean anything, she wished to know it. He would never, never marry her,—wouldn't he? Or, possibly, her question was but part of a plan, or general campaign, on her part, to test his sanity? Six persons—real competents, too!— had affirmed that he wasn't "just right." Be that as it may, Miss Gerald dropped this bomb in Master Bob's camp and waited the effect with mien serene.

Her query worked the expected havoc, all right. Bob's jaw fell. Then his eyes began to flash with a new fierce love-light. He couldn't help it. Marry her?—Great Scott!—She, asking him, if he would? He felt his pulses beating faster and the blood pumping in his veins. His arms went out—very eager, strong, primitive arms they looked— that cave-man kind! Arms that seize resistless maidens and enfold them, willy-nilly! Miss Gerald really should have felt much alarmed, especially as there was so much doubt as to Bob's sanity. It's bad enough to be alone with an ordinary crazy man, but a crazy man who is in love with one? That is calculated to be a rather unusual and thrilling experience.

However, though Miss Gerald may have entertained a few secret fears and possible regrets for her own somewhat mad precipitancy, she managed to maintain a fair semblance of composure. She had the courage to "stand by" the coup. She was like a tall lily that seems to hold itself unafraid before the breaking of the tempest. She did not even draw back, though she threw her head back slightly. And in her eyes was a challenge. Not a love challenge, though Bob could not discern that! His own gaze was too blurred.

Miss Gerald suddenly drew in her breath quickly, as one who felt she would need her courage now. Almost had Bob, in that moment of forgetfulness, drawn her into his arms and so completed the paradoxical picture of himself, when the impulse was abruptly arrested. He seemed suddenly to awaken to a saner comprehension of the requirements of the moment. His arms fell to his side.

"That's a joke, of course," he said hoarsely.

"And if it wasn't?" she challenged him. There was mockery now in her eyes, and her figure had relaxed.

"You affirm it isn't?"

"I said *if* it wasn't?"

"I guess you win," said Bob wearily. These extremes of emotion were wearing on the system.

"You mean you wouldn't, even if I had really, actually—?"

"I mean you certainly do know how to 'even up' with a chap. When he doesn't dare dream of heaven, you suddenly pretend to fling open the golden gates and invite him to enter."

"Like St. Peter," said the girl.

"Ah, you *are* laughing," said Bob bitterly, and dropped his head. Her assurance was regal. "As if it wasn't hard enough, anyway, to get you out of my darn-fool head," he murmured reproachfully.

"Then you reject me?" said the girl, moving toward the entrance. "Good! I mean, bad! So humiliating to have been rejected! Good night, Mr. Bennett. No—it isn't necessary for you to accompany me to the house. I really couldn't think of troubling you after your unkind refusal to—"

Bob groaned. "I say, there is always your aunt, you know, who can ask me to vacate the—" he called out.

"I'll think about it," said the lady. A faint perfume was wafted past him and the vision vanished. Bob sank down on the cold marble seat.

He remained thus for some time, oblivious to the world, when another car, en route from the village to the house, purred past him, spitting viciously, however, between purrs. Bob didn't even look around. Spit!—spit!—purr!—purr!—Its two lights were like the eyes of some monster pussy-cat, on the war-path for trouble. Spit!—it seemed in a horribly vicious mood. More "spits" than "purrs," now! Then the car stopped, though it was some distance from the house.

"Curse this old rattletrap!" said a man's voice.

"Oh, I guess no one'll pay any attention to it," spoke another occupant. "Besides, it was the only one to be had at the station, and we had to get here quick."

"You bet! The quicker, the better," observed a third man.

They all got out, not far from where Bob sat in the dark gazing into a void, but he did not notice. Cars might come, and cars might go, for all of him. He was dimly aware of the sound of voices but he had no interest in guests, newly-arrived or otherwise. One of the trio paid the driver of the car and it purred back, somewhat less viciously, from whence it came.

"Better separate when we get near the house and approach it carefully," said the first speaker in low tense tones. "We've got to get hold of him without anybody knowing it."

"That's right. Wouldn't do to let *them*"—with significant accent—"know what we've come for," said the second man. The trio were quite out of ear-shot of Bob, by now.

"Hope it'll turn out all right," spoke the third anxiously. "Why, in heaven's name, didn't we think of this in the first place?"

"Can't think of every contingency!" answered the first speaker viciously. "Our plan now is to get hold of one of the servants. A nice fat tip, and then—Come on! No time to waste!"

As they made their way up the driveway to the house Bob looked drearily around. His eyes noted and mechanically followed the trio of dark forms. He saw them stop near the house; then he observed one approach a side window and peer in. A moment later another approached another window and peered in.

"That's funny!" thought Bob, without any particular emotion. At the same time, he recalled that a band of burglars had been going about, looting country-houses. Perhaps these fellows were after a few hundred thousand dollars' worth of jewels? There might be half a million dollars' worth of jewelry sprinkled about among Mrs. Ralston's guests. But what did it matter? The presence of these intruders seemed too trifling a matter to think about now, and Bob sank into another reverie.

How long he remained thus, he did not know. The laughter and talk of a number of guests, coming out the front way (end of a "trot," probably) aroused him and Bob got up.

As he did so, he fancied he saw again the three men he had noticed, then forgotten, slip around toward the back of the house. Throughout the gardens, the moonlight made clear spots on the ground where the bright rays sifted through the foliage or shone down between the trees, and they had to skip across one of these bright places to get around somewhere behind the big mansion. Undoubtedly, the appearance from the house of the guests who wanted to cool off had startled the intruders and inspired a desire to make themselves less conspicuous for the time being. Bob entertained a vague impression that the conduct of the trio was rather crude and amateurish, though that didn't worry him. He didn't care whether they were full-fledged yeggmen of the smoothest class, or only bungling artists, a discredit to their profession. He dismissed consideration of them as quickly again as he had done before.

A yawn escaped his lips, and it rather surprised him that a broken-hearted man could yawn. He looked at his watch, holding it in the moonlight, and saw that it was late enough now so that he could retire if he wished, without violating, to any great degree, that even-tenor-of-his-way clause. Accordingly Bob got up and walked toward the house. A side door was open and he went in that way and up to his room. He was glad he didn't encounter any one—that is, any one he had to speak to. The monocle-man drifted by him somewhere, but Bob didn't have to pay much attention to him. He could imagine the superior way in which the Britisher had informed Miss Gerald that he found him (Bob) an "interesting young man." The monocle-man and the bishop seemed to agree on that point.

Undressing hastily, Bob flung himself into bed. He had gone through so much he was tired and scarcely had he touched the sheets when the welcoming arms of Morpheus claimed him. His sleep was sound—very sound! In fact, it was so sound that something occurred and he didn't know it. It occurred again—several times—and still he did not know it. Another interval!—a long one! Bob yet slept the sleep of the overwrought. His fagged brain was trying to readjust itself. He could have slept right through to the dawn, but this was not to be. Long before the glowing god made its appearance in the east, Bob was rudely yanked from the arms of Morpheus.

CHAPTER IX—ANOTHER SURPRISE

Three men were in his room and Bob found himself sitting up in bed and blinking at them. The lights they had turned on seemed rather bright.

"Hello!" said Bob.

"Hello yourself!" said the commodore in a low but nasty manner. "And not so loud!"

"Some sleeper, you are!" spoke Dickie in a savage whisper.

"Believe he heard, all right!" came Clarence's hushed, unamiable tones. "Perverse beast, and pretended not to!"

Bob hugged his knees with his arms. "You've torn your pants," he observed to the commodore.

"Never you mind *that*" as guardedly, though no more pleasantly than before.

"Oh, all right," said Bob meekly. He didn't ask any questions, nor did he exhibit any curiosity. There couldn't anything happen now that would make matters much worse. But in that, he was "reckoning without his host."

"Got in the window, of course," he observed in a low unconcerned tone, as if their coming and being there after midnight was the most natural occurrence in the world. "Not so hard to get in, with that balcony out there. All you had to do was to 'shin up' and then there's that trellis to help. Good strong trellis, too. Regular Jacob's ladder! Easiest thing for burglars! Thought you *were* burglars," he added contemplatively.

"You mean you saw us?" snapped the commodore, almost forgetting his caution. His expression matched his tone. He was no longer the jovial sailorman; he wore now a regular Dick Deadeye look. To Bob's comprehensive glance he appeared like a fragment in a revival of *Pinafore*.

"Oh, I didn't know it was you," said Bob.

"Where were you?"

"Summer-house."

"Think of that," murmured the commodore, disgustedly. "Bird at hand, and we didn't know it. Fool of a bird had to hop away and make us all this trouble!"

"I told you I thought you were burglars," observed Bob patiently. He didn't care how they abused him or what names they called him.

That disagreeable look on Dan's face was replaced by a startled one. "Good gracious, man"—only that wasn't the expression he used— "I hope you haven't told any one you saw burglars prowling around? Nice for us if you did!" As he spoke he gazed anxiously toward the window, before which they had taken the precaution to draw a heavy drape after entering.

"No, I didn't tell a soul."

"But—I don't understand why you didn't when you thought—?"

"I ought to have spoken, I suppose," said Bob with a melancholy smile. "But it didn't seem very important and—I guess I forgot. These little jewel robberies are getting to be such commonplace occurrences!"

The commodore stared at him. Then he touched his forehead. "A lot of trouble you've made for us," he said, speaking in that low tense voice, while Clarence and Dickie looked on in mad and reproachful fashion. "Bribed a servant to tell you to slip out! Told him to whisper that we were waiting in the garden and simply had to see you at once! Didn't you hear him rap on your door?"

"No," answered Bob sorrowfully.

"Heavens, man! believe you'd sleep through an earthquake and cyclone combined! Servant came back and told us he'd tapped on your door as loudly as he dared. Was afraid he'd arouse the whole house if he knocked louder. When you leave a 'call' at the hotels, how do they manage? Break down the door with an ax?"

Bob overlooked the sarcasm. The commodore might have thumped him with an ax, at the moment, and he wouldn't have protested very hard. He murmured a contrite apology.

"Get my telegram?" said the commodore.

"Yes. What *could* you have been thinking about when you sent it? How could I leave when I had to stay? Thought you must have been sailing pretty close in the wind at the yacht club, when you dashed it off! Could just feel your main-sail fluttering."

The commodore swore softly but effectively. Clarence and Dickie murmured something, too. Bob hugged his knees closer. Being so unhappy himself, he couldn't but feel a dull sympathy when he saw any one else put out.

"See here," said the commodore, "what's the situation? We never dreamed, of course, that you would come here. Have you been talking with Mrs. Dan and Mrs. Clarence? Dickie's been conjuring all kinds of awful things you might have told them, if they cornered you and you got that truth-telling stunt going. Dickie's got an imagination. Too confounded much imagination!" Here the commodore wiped his brow. That was quite a bad tear in his pants but he appeared oblivious to it. "Maybe you would have thought it a capital way to turn the tables on us poor chaps?" he went on, stabbing Bob with a baleful look. "Perhaps you came here on purpose?"

"No," said Bob, "I couldn't have done that, of course, owing to the conditions." And he related what had happened to bring him there.

Dan groaned. "Why, it was we, ourselves, who steered him right up against her at the Waldorf. It was we who got him asked down here. I suppose you've been chuckling ever since you came?" Turning on Bob, with a correct imitation of Mr. Deadeye, at his grouchiest moment.

"No," said Bob, speaking to immeasurable distance, "I haven't done any chuckling since I came here. Nary a chuckle!"

"Let's get down to brass tacks," interrupted Dickie, "and learn if our worst apprehensions are realized. There's a girl down here I think a lot of and I'd like to know if, by any chance, any conversation you may have had with her turned on me. I allude to Miss Dolly—"

"Hold on," said the commodore. "That's not very important. Suppose she should have found out a few things about you? You aren't married. It's different in the case of married men, like Clarence and me here. We'll dismiss Miss Dolly, if you please, for the present—"

"I really haven't said anything to Miss Dolly about you," said Bob to Dickie. "Your name hasn't been mentioned between us." He was glad he could reassure one of them, at least. He wouldn't have had Dickie so sorrowful as himself for the world.

That young man looked immensely relieved. It may be he experienced new hope of leading the temperamental young thing to the altar, and incidentally consummating a consolidation of competing chimneys, conveniently contiguous. "Thanks, old chap," he said, and shook Bob's hand heartily.

"But what about us?" whispered the commodore sibilantly. "Have you talked with Mrs. Clarence or Mrs. Dan to any great extent?"

"I haven't had hardly a word with Mrs. Clarence," answered Bob, whereupon Clarence began to "throw out his chest," the way Dickie had done.

The commodore shifted uneasily, seeming to find difficulty in continuing the conversation. He moved back and forth once or twice, but realizing he was making a slight noise, stood still again, and looked down at Bob.

"Talk much with Mrs. Dan?" he at length asked nervously.

"I did have a little conversation with Mrs. Dan," Bob was forced to reply. "Or, I should say, to be strictly truthful, rather a long conversation. You see, I took her in to dinner."

The commodore showed signs of weakness. He seemed to have very indecisive legs all of a sudden. "Talk about me?" he managed to ejaculate.

"Some. I'm not certain just how much."

"What—what was said?"

"I can't remember all. It's very confused. I've had a lot of conversations, you see, and most of them awfully unpleasant. I remember, though, that Mrs. Dan impressed me as a very broad-minded lady. Said she had lived in Paris, and was not a bit jealous."

"What!" Dan was breathing hard.

"Said she always wanted you to have the best kind of a time."

"Did she say that?" asked the commodore. "And you believed it? Go on." In a choked voice. "Did you tell her about that cabaret evening?"

"I believe it was mentioned, incidentally."

"Say *I* was there?" put in Clarence quickly. He was losing that "chestiness."

"I rather think I did. I—what is that?" Bob looked toward the window. There was a sound below at the foot of the balcony. Some one turned out the light in the room and Bob strode to the window and looked out. "It's a dog," he said. "He's snuffing around at the foot."

"He's doing more than snuffing," observed the commodore apprehensively, as at that moment a bark smote the air. They stood motionless and silent. The dog stopped barking, but went on snuffing. Maybe it would go away after a moment, and they waited. Dickie and the commodore had thrashed out that question of dogs. With so many guests around, they had figured that, of course, they would be dog-safe. Didn't they look like guests? How could a dog tell the difference between them and a guest? It is true, they hadn't been expecting so much trouble as they had been put to, to find Bob. They had, in that little balcony-climbing feat, rather exceeded what they had expected to be called on to do. In their impatience, they had acted somewhat impetuously, but it had looked just as easy, after the servant had pointed out the room and told them Bob was in, as certain sounds from his bed indubitably indicated.

They couldn't very well enter the house as self-invited guests, though they, of course, would have been made welcome. They couldn't very well say they had all changed their minds about those original invitations which had naturally included husbands as well as wives. After all three had declined to come on account of business, it would certainly look like collusion, if all three found they hadn't had urgent business, at all, in town. If anything untoward or disastrous had happened in the conversational line, with Bob as the Demon God, Truth, their sudden entrance upon the stage of festivities, would seem to partake of inner perturbation; it might even appear to be a united and concentrated case of triple guilty conscience. This, obviously, must be avoided at any cost. How they had heard Bob was here at the Ralston house, matters not. Naturally they had kept tab on his movements, where he went and what he did being of some moment to them.

The dog barked again. Thereupon, a window opened and they knew that some one had been aroused.

"He's looking out. It's the monocle-chap," whispered Bob.

"Who's he?"

"One of Mrs. Ralston's importations. Belonged to that Anglo-English colony when she did that little emigration act in dear old London."

"Hang it, we've got to get out," whispered the commodore nervously. No matter what had been said; no matter what the Demon God of Truth had done, it was incumbent on them not to remain longer, with that dog looking up toward Bob's window and making that spasmodic racket. Some one might get up and go out and see footprints, or a disturbed trellis. The commodore forgot a certain desperate business proposition, apropos of that confounded wager, he had come to put to Bob. That infernal dog got on his nerves and put that other matter, which would settle this truth-telling stunt at once, right out of his mind.

It was all very well, however, to say they "had to get out," but it was another matter to tell how they were going to do it. They couldn't descend the way they had come, and meet doggie. Bob arose to the occasion.

"I can let you into the hall and show you downstairs, to that side door on the other side of the house. You can take one of my golf sticks, just as a safeguard, but I think you'll be able to circumvent the jolly little barker without being obliged to use it."

"What kind of a dog is it?" whispered the commodore who had a pronounced aversion to canines.

"Looked like a smallish dog. Might be a bull."

"Better give us each a club," suggested Clarence in a weak voice.

Which Bob did. The dog renewed the vocal performance, and— "Hurry," whispered the commodore. "Find means to communicate with you to-morrow, Mr. Bennett." Bob didn't resent the formality of this designation, which implied to what depths he had fallen in good old Dan's estimation. "Can we get down-stairs without any one hearing us?"

Bob thought they could. Anyhow, they would have to try, so he opened the door softly and led the way. Fortunately, the house was solidly built and not creaky. They attained down-stairs safely, and at last reached the side door without causing any disturbance. Bob unfastened the door, the key turned noiselessly and they looked out. There was no sign of any living thing on lawn or garden on this side of the house.

"Out you go quickly," murmured Bob, glancing apprehensively over his shoulder. His position was not a particularly agreeable one. Suppose one of the servants, on an investigating tour as to the cause of doggie's perturbation, should chance upon him (Bob) showing three men out of the house in that secret manner at this time of night?

But before disappearing into the night, the commodore took time to whisper: "Was Gee-gee's name mentioned?"

"I fear so," said Bob sadly.

The commodore wasted another second or two to tell Bob fiercely what he thought of him and how they would "fix" him on the morrow, after which he sprang out and darted away like a rabbit.

Bob wanted to call out that they were welcome to "fix" him, but he was afraid that others beside Dan might hear him, so he closed and locked the door carefully and stood there alone in the great hall, in his dressing-gown. Then he sat down in a dark corner and listened. Better wait until all was quiet, he told himself, before retracing his steps to his room. The dog seemed to have stopped barking altogether now and soon any persons it might have awakened would be asleep again. His trio of visitors must be well on their way to the village by this time, he thought. He was sorry the commodore seemed to feel so bad. And Clarence?—poor Clarence! That last look of his haunted Bob. Anyhow, he was pleased Dickie had, so far, escaped his (Bob's) devastating touch.

How long he sat there he did not know. Probably only a few moments. A big clock ticked near by, which was the only sound now to be heard. Suddenly it occurred to him that he had better return to his room, and wearily he arose. Up-stairs it seemed darker than it had been when he had left his room. He had the dim lights in the great hall below to guide him then. Now it was a little more difficult. However, after traversing without mishap a few gloomy corridors— he realized what a big house it really was—he reached, at last, his room near the end of one of the upper halls and entered.

He had a vague idea he had left his door partly ajar, but he wasn't sure; probably he hadn't, for it was now closed; or maybe a draft of air had closed it. Groping his way in the dark for his bed, he ran against a chair. This ruffled his temper somewhat as the sharp edge had come in contact with that sensitive part of the anatomy, known as the shin-bone. He felt for his bed, but it wasn't there where it ought to be. He must have got turned around coming in. His fingers ran over a dresser. Some of the articles on it seemed strange to him. He thought he heard a rustle and stood still, with senses alert, experiencing a regular burglar-feeling at the moment. He hadn't become so ossified to emotion as he had supposed. But everything was now as silent as the grave. Again his hand swept out, to learn where he was, and again his fingers swept over the dresser. What were all those confounded things? He didn't know he had left so much loose junk lying around. And where was that confounded switch-button?

At that moment some one else found it, for the room became suddenly flooded with light. Bob started back, and as he did so, something fell from the dresser to the floor. He stared toward the bed in amazement and horror. Some one, with the clothes drawn up about her, was sitting up. Bob wasn't the only one who had a surprise that night. The temperamental, little dark thing was treated to one, too. Above the white counterpane, she stared at Bob.

CHAPTER X—INTO BONDAGE

She continued to stare for some moments, while he stood frozen to the spot. Then the young lady's face changed. Fear, startled wonder, gave way to an expression of growing comprehension and into her eyes came such an excited look.

"You!" said Miss Dolly in a thrilling whisper. And then—"Pick it up, please."

Instead of picking anything up—he didn't know what—Bob was about to rush for the door, when— "Stop! Or I'll scream," exclaimed Miss Dolly. "I'll scream so loud I'll wake every one in the house."

Bob stopped. In his eyes was an agony of contrition and shame. Miss Dolly, however, seemed quite self-possessed. She might have been frightened at first, but she was no longer that. Her temperamental, somewhat childish face wore a thrill of pleasurable anticipation. "Now pick it up," she repeated.

"What?" stammered Bob in a shrinking voice.

"The brooch, to be sure. Didn't you drop it?"

"I?" said Bob, drawing his dressing-gown closer about him. They were speaking in stage whispers.

"Of course. Wasn't it what you came for?"

"Came for? Great heavens!—Do you think?—"

"Think?" said Miss Dolly. "I know."

Bob looked at her. Her face appeared elf-like, uncannily wise. But for all her outward calm, her eyes were great big, excited eyes. His horrified glance turned quickly from them to regard a gleaming diamond and pearl brooch on the rug. "Jumping Je-hoshaphat! You don't think I'm—"

"One of those thrilling society-highwaymen, or social buccaneers?" said Miss Dolly. "Of course, and I'm so glad it happened like this. I wouldn't have missed it for the world. Really, I've always wanted to meet one of those popular heroes. And now to think my dream has come true! It's just like a play, isn't it?"

"It is not," replied Bob savagely. This was too much. It was just about the last straw. "I—" Then he stopped. Suppose any one should hear him? Miss Dolly's temperamental and comprehensive eyes read his thought.

"I don't think there's any danger," she purred soothingly. "You see there's a bathroom on one side of the room and a brick wall on the other. I wouldn't be surprised if all the rooms are separated by brick partitions," she confided to him. "Mrs. Ralston likes everything perfect—sound-proof, fire-proof, and all that."

"See here," said Bob. "I was just wandering around—couldn't sleep—and—and I came in here, quite by mistake. Thought it was my own room!" With some vehemence.

Miss Dolly shook her head reprovingly, and her temperamental hair flowed all about her over the white counterpane. She knew it must look very becoming, it was such wonderful hair—that is, for dark hair. Bob preferred light. Not that he was thinking of hair, now! "Can't you do better than that?" asked the temperamental young thing.

"Better than what?" queried Bob ill-naturedly. He was beginning to feel real snappy.

"Invent a better whopper, I mean?"

"It isn't a whopper, and—and I positively refuse to stay here any longer. Positively!"

"Oh, no; not positively," said Miss Dolly, nodding a wise young head. "You're going to stay, unless—you know the alternative. Since I'm destined to be a heroine, I want a regular play-scene. I don't want my part cut down to nothing. Don't you love thief-plays, Mr. Bennett? It's such fun to see people running around, not knowing who *is* the thief. I'm sure I feel quite privileged, in this instance."

Bob growled beneath his breath. He was handsome enough certainly for a matinee hero. He was tall and lithe and had such clean-cut features. The temperamental young thing regarded him with thrilling approval. He entirely realized her ideal of a social burglar. It seemed almost too good to be true.

"I knew you were different from other men," she said. "Something told me from the very first; perhaps it was the way you tangoed. I expected you would ask me to trot, but you didn't." Reprovingly. "Suppose you were otherwise engaged?" Glancing toward the brooch.

"Not the way you think!" said Bob gloomily, looking more striking than ever in that melancholy pose. It seemed to harmonize with a crime-stained career.

"Of course," murmured Dolly, "it was you who got Mrs. Templeton Blenfield's wonderful emeralds?"

"It was not," answered Bob curtly.

"You were at that costume ball where she lost them?"

"Suppose I was?" he snapped. Yes, snapped! There is a limit to human endurance.

"And you were at Mrs. Benton Briscoe's when a tiara mysteriously disappeared?"

"Well, I'm hanged!" said Bob, staring at her.

"Oh, I hope not—that is, I hope you won't be, some day," answered Dolly. "Are you going to 'fess up?' You'd better. Maybe I won't betray you—yet. Maybe I won't at all, if you're real nice."

"Oh!" said Bob. Whereupon she smiled at him sweetly, just as if to say it was nice and exciting to have a great, big, bold (and wildly handsome) society-highwayman in her power. Why, she could send him to jail, if she wanted to. She had but to lift a little finger and he would have to jump. The consciousness of guilty knowledge and power she possessed made her glow all over. She didn't really know though, yet, whether she would be kind or severe.

"Do you operate alone, or with accomplices?" she asked, after a few moments' pleasurable anticipations.

"I beg pardon?" Bob was again gazing uneasily toward the door.

"Got any pals?" She tried to talk the way they do in the thief-books.

"No, I haven't," snapped Bob. That truth pact made it necessary to answer the most silly questions.

"Well, I didn't know but you had," murmured the temperamental young thing. "I heard a dog barking and that made me think you might have them. You're sure you didn't let anybody into the house?"

"I didn't."

Miss Dolly snuggled herself together more cozily. She seemed about to ask some more questions. Perhaps she would want to know if he had let anybody out, and then he would have to tell her—

"Look here," said Bob desperately. "Maybe it hasn't occurred to you, but—this—this isn't exactly proper. Me here, like this, and you—"

"Oh, I'm not afraid," answered Miss Dolly with wonderful assurance. "I can quite take care of myself."

"But—but—" more desperately—"if I should be discovered?— Can't you see, for your own sake—?"

"My own sake?" The big innocent eyes opened wider. "In that case, of course, I'd tell them the truth."

"The truth!" How he hated the word! "You mean that I—?" Glancing toward the brooch.

"Of course!" Tranquilly.

Bob tried to consider. He could see what would happen to him, if they were interrupted. It certainly was a most preposterous conversation, anyhow. Besides, it wasn't the place or the time for a conversation of any kind. He had just about made up his mind that he would go, whether she screamed or not, and take the consequences, however disagreeable they might be, when—

"Well, trot along," said Miss Dolly graciously. "I suppose you've got a lot of work to do to-night and it's rather unkind to detain you. Only pick up the brooch before you go." He obeyed. "Now put it on the dresser and leave it there. Hard to do that, isn't it?"

"No, it isn't." Savagely.

"Well, you can go now. By the way, Mrs. Vanderpool has a big bronze-colored diamond surrounded by wonderful pink pearls. It's an antique and—would adorn a connoisseur's collection."

"But I tell you I am not—"

"My! How stupid, to keep on saying that! But, of course, you must really be very clever. Society-highwaymen always are. Good night. So glad I was thinking of something else and forgot to lock the door!"

Bob went to the door and she considerately waited until he had reached it; then she put out a hand and pushed a convenient button which shut off the light. Bob opened the door but closed it quickly again. He fancied he saw some one out there in the hall, a shadowy form in the distance, but was not absolutely sure.

"Aren't you gone?" said the temperamental young thing.

"S-sh!" said Bob.

For some moments there was silence, thrilling enough, even for her. Then Bob gently opened the door once more, though very slightly, and peered out of the tiniest crack, but he failed to see any one now, so concluded he must have been mistaken. The shadows were most deceptive. Anyhow, there was more danger in staying than in going, so he slid out and closed the door. At the same moment he heard a very faint click. It seemed to come from the other side of the hall. He didn't like that, he told himself, and waited to make sure no one was about. The ensuing silence reassured him somewhat; and the "click," he argued, might have come from the door he himself had closed.

The temperamental young thing, holding her breath, heard him now move softly but swiftly away. She listened, nothing happened. Then she stretched her young form luxuriously and pondered on the delirious secret that was all hers. A secret that made Bob her slave! Abjectly her slave! Like the servant of the lamp! She could compel him to turn somersaults if she wanted to.

Bob awoke with a slight headache, which, however, didn't surprise him any. He only wondered his head didn't ache more. People came down to breakfast almost any time, and sometimes they didn't come down at all but sipped coffee in their rooms, continental-fashion. It was late when Bob got up, so a goodly number of the guests—the exceptions including Mrs. Dan and Mrs. Clarence—were down by the time he sauntered into the big sun-room, where breakfast was served to all with American appetites.

The temperamental little thing managed accidentally (?) to encounter him at the doorway before he got into the room with the others. He shivered slightly when he saw her, though she looked most attractive in her rather bizarre way. Bob gazed beyond her, however, to a vision in the window. "Vision!" That just described what Miss Gwendoline looked like, with the sunlight on her and making an aureole of her glorious fair hair. Of course one could put an adjective or two, before the "vision"—such as "beautiful," or something even stronger—without being accused of extravagance.

The little dark thing, uttering some platitude, followed Bob's look, but she didn't appear jealous. She hadn't quite decided how much latitude to give Bob. That young gentleman noticed that the hammer-thrower, looking like one of those stalwart, masculine tea-passers in an English novel, was not far from Miss Gwendoline. His big fingers could apparently handle delicate china as well as mighty iron balls or sledges. He comported himself as if his college education had included a course at Tuller's in Oxford Street, in London, where six-foot guardsmen are taught to maneuver among spindle-legged tables and to perform almost impossible feats without damage to crockery.

Miss Dolly now maneuvered so as to draw Bob aside in the hall to have a word or two before he got to bacon and eggs. What she said didn't improve his appetite.

"I'm so disappointed in you," she began in a low voice.

He asked why, though not because he really cared to know.

"After that hint of mine!" she explained reproachfully. "About Mrs. Vanderpool's bronze diamond, I mean!"

"I fear I do not understand you," said Bob coldly.

She bent nearer. "Of course I thought it would disappear," she murmured. "I expected you to execute one of those clever coups, and so I went purposely to Mrs. Vanderpool's room on some pretext this morning to learn if it was gone. But it wasn't. I cleverly led the conversation up to it and she showed it to me."

"Great Scott!" he exclaimed. "Did you think she wouldn't have it to show you? That it had found its way to my pockets?"

"Of course," she answered. "And you *are* quite sure you haven't it, after all?" she asked suspiciously.

"How could I, when you saw—"

"Oh, you might have substituted a counterfeit brooch just like it for—"

Bob groaned. "You certainly have absorbed those plays," he remarked.

"I expected a whole lot of things would be gone," she went on, "and, apparently," with disappointment, "no one has missed anything. It's quite tame. Did you get discouraged because you failed to land the 'loot'—is that the word?—in my case? And did you then just go prosaically to bed?"

"I certainly went to bed, though there was nothing prosaic about the procedure."

"And yet what a dull night it must have been for you!"

"I shouldn't call it that."

"No?" She shifted the conversation. "Who do you suppose has come? Dickie Donnelly. Said he had arrived in town on some business and took advantage of the opportunity to make a little call on me. Incidentally, he seems interested in you. Said he would make it a point to see you after you got down. He's out on the veranda smoking now, I guess. He wanted to talk to me but I made an excuse to shoo him away. He isn't half so exciting as you are, you know. I'm quite positive now I couldn't marry him and annex his old chimneys to ours, for all the world. Chimneys are such commonplace means to a livelihood, Mr. Bennett, don't you think? They are so ugly and dependable. Not at all romantic and precarious! They just smoke and you get richer. There isn't a single thrill in a whole forest of chimneys. But I mustn't really keep you from your breakfast any longer," she added with sudden sedulousness. "I've quite planned what we're going to do to-day."

"You have?" With a slight accent on the first word.

"Yes," she assured him quietly. "So run along now."

The slave, glad to get away, started to obey, when—"One moment!" said Miss Dolly as if seized with an afterthought. "Dickie asked about you so particularly that it occurred to me that— Well, do you think he harbors any suspicions?"

"Suspicions?"

"Yes; do you imagine he, too, by any chance, may have guessed— you know?" And Dolly again drew closer, her eyes beaming with new excitement.

Bob looked disagreeable, but he had to reply. "I'm sure he doesn't think what you do," he answered ill-humoredly.

Dolly looked relieved, but still slightly dubious. She didn't appear to notice that lack of appreciation in Bob's manner for her interest in his welfare. "Well, you'd better see him," she said in the tone of one who had already established herself to the post of secret adviser. "He's bent on an interview with you. Says it's business. And speaking about business, what business could he possibly have in that dinky little town? Unless he wanted to buy the whole village! His conduct is, to say the least, slightly mysterious. Dickie may prove a factor to be reckoned with."

"That's true enough," assented Bob, and went in to breakfast.

The temperamental little thing gazed after him approvingly; she quite gloried in her big burglar. It was so nice to know something no one else knew, to be a little wiser than all the rest of the world, including the police and the detective force! Bob must be terribly resourceful and subtle, to have deceived them all so thoroughly. He only seemed a little dense at times, just to keep up the deception. It was a part of the role. He wouldn't even let her, who knew his secret, see under the surface and she liked him all the better for his reticence. It lent piquancy to the situation and added zest to the game. Dickie's manner had certainly seemed to her unduly sober. He appeared to have something on his mind, though of course he was awfully eager and joyous about seeing her.

At the breakfast-table Bob only dallied with his hot rolls and took but a few gulps of coffee. The monocle-man who sat near by noticed that want of appetite.

"Don't seem very keen for your feed this morning," he observed jocularly.

"No, not over-peckish," answered Bob.

"Why not? You look—aw—fit enough!" Reaching for one of those racks for unbuttered toast which Mrs. Ralston had brought home with her from London.

"Headache, for one thing," returned Bob. It was the truth, or part of the truth. No one looked sympathetic, however. In fact, with the exception of the monocle-man (Mrs. Ralston hadn't yet come down), every one in there made it apparent he or she desired as little as possible of Mr. Bennett's society. Bob soon got up, casting a last bitter glance at Miss Gerald who seemed quite contented with her stalwart, honest-looking hammer-thrower. And why not? His character, Bob reflected, was unimpeachable. He looked so good and honest and so utterly wholesome that Bob, who himself was tainted with suspicion, wanted to get out of his presence. So Bob went out to the porch, to hunt up Dickie and ascertain what was the matter with him?

It didn't take Bob long to learn what was worrying Dickie. He was carrying the weight of a new and tremendous responsibility. He had now become an emissary, a friend in need, to Clarence and the commodore, who certainly needed one at this moment. It seemed that Mrs. Clarence and Mrs. Dan had set detectives searching for Gee-gee and Gid-up and they had succeeded in locating one of the pair, partly by a freckle and a turned-up nose. The detectives must have worked fast. They were assisted by the fact that foolish Clarence had kept up an innocent and Platonic friendship with "Gee-gee's" chum, after that momentous evening when Bob had been along. Now when a young man begins to hang around the vicinity of a stage door in a big car, he is apt to make himself a subject for remark and to become known, especially to the door-keeper who takes a fatherly interest in his Shetland herd. As Gid-up and Gee-gee were inseparable, it was but a step to place one by the other.

Detectives, Dickie informed Bob, had already interviewed the ladies. They may have offered them money in exchange for information. Mrs. Dan was very rich in her own name. She could outbid the commodore. Gid-up might hesitate or refuse to supply or manufacture information for filthy lucre, but Gee-gee was known to be ambitious. She longed to soar. And here was a means to that end. Quite a legitimate and customary one!

"Why, that girl would do anything to get herself talked about," said Dickie sadly, thinking of Dan, and incidentally, too, of Clarence. "She'd manufacture information by the car-load. Out of a little, teeny-weeny remnant of truth, she'd build a magnificent divorce case. Think of the glorious publicity! Why, Gee-gee and one of the manager-chaps would sit up nights to see how many columns they could fill each day in the press. They'd make poor old Dan out worse than Nero. They'd picture him as a monster. They'd give him claws. And Clarence would come crawling after him like a slimy snake. Incidentally, they'd throw in a few weeps for Gee-gee. And then some more for Gid-up! Why, man, when I think of the mischief you've done—"

"Me?" said Bob miserably, almost overwhelmed by this pathetic picture Dickie had drawn. "But it wasn't! It was Truth." Dickie snorted. "What do you want me to do? Commit suicide? Annihilate truth? That would be one way of doing it. I'm sure I shouldn't much mind. Shall I poison Truth or blow its brains out? Or shall I take it down to the lake and jump in with it? Do you think it has made *me* very happy? What am I? What have I become? Where is my good name?" He was thinking of what the temperamental little thing considered him. "Say, do I look like a criminal?" he demanded, confronting Dickie. The latter stared, then shrugged. Of course, if Bob wanted to rave—? "Or a crazy man? Do I look crazy?" he continued almost fiercely. "Well, there are people in there," indicating the house, "who think I am." Dickie started slightly and looked thoughtful. "You ask the judge, or the doctor, or—a lot of others. Ask Miss Gwendoline Gerald," he concluded bitterly.

Dickie shifted a leg. "It might not be a bad idea," he said in a peculiar tone, whose accent Bob didn't notice, however. For some moments the two young men sat moodily and silently side by side.

"Where are Dan and Clarence now?" asked Bob in a dull tone, after a while.

"Gone to New York. Hustled there early this morning after some hurry-up messages gave an inkling of what was going on. I'm to do my best at this end. Keep my eyes on Mrs. Dan and Mrs. Clarence, and incidentally, learn and do what I can."

As he spoke Dickie tapped his leg with his cane; at the same time he bestowed another of those peculiar looks on Bob. Just then a young lady stepped from the house and came toward them. She was in the trimmest attire—for shooting or fishing—and looked extraordinarily trim, herself. A footman followed with two light rods and a basket.

"Come on," she said lightly to Bob. "Might as well get started. It's almost noon."

"Started?" he stammered, staring at her.

"Yes, on that fishing excursion we planned."

"We?" he repeated in the same tone. And then— "All right!" he said. It occurred to him, if he went off somewhere alone, with the temperamental young thing, he wouldn't, at any rate, have to bob against a score or so of other people throughout the day. Better one than a crowd! "I'm ready," he added, taking the rods and small basket.

"But, I say—" Dickie had arisen. There was a new look in his eyes— of disappointment, surprise—perhaps apprehension, too! "I say—" he repeated, looking darkly toward Bob.

The temperamental young thing threw him a smile. "Sorry, Dickie, but a previous engagement.—You know how it is!"

"I can imagine," thought Dickie ominously, watching them disappear. Then his glance shifted viciously toward the house, and there was a look of stern determination in his eyes. As he mingled with others of the guests a few moments later, however, his expression had become one of studied amiability. Dickie was deep. His grievance now was as great as Dan's or Clarence's.

CHAPTER XI—FISHING

They had an afternoon of it, Bob and Dolly. Bob made himself useful, if not agreeable. He was a willing though not altogether cheerful slave. But the girl did not appear to mind that. She had spirits enough for both of them and ordered Bob around royally. She was nice to him, but she wanted him to know that he was her property, as much hers as if she had bought him at one of those old human auction sales. Only hers was a white slave!

She had the grandest time. She made him help her across the stream on a number of unnecessary occasions, holding the slave's hand, so that she wouldn't slip on the slippery stones. And once she had him carry her across. She had to, because there weren't any stones, slippery or otherwise, she could avail herself of, at that particular spot. It is true she might have gone on a little farther and found some slippery stones that would have served her purpose, but she pretended not to know about them. Besides, what is the use of being a despot and having a private slave, all to yourself, if you don't use him and make him work? Mr. Bennett wasn't only a slave either, he was a romantic hero, as well, and in the books, heroes always carry the heroines across streams. Miss Dolly experienced a real bookish feeling when Bob carried her. He fully realized the popular ideal, he had such strong arms. True, he didn't breathe on her neck, or in her ear, and he grasped her rather gingerly, but she found no fault over that. Her great big hero was a modest hero. But he was very manly and masculine, too.

He had plunged right in the stream, shoes and all, in spite of her suggestion that he had better take them off. But what cared he for wet feet? Might cause pneumonia, of course; but pneumonia had no terrors for Bob! She smiled at his precipitancy, while secretly approving of it. The act partook of a large gallantry. It reminded her of Sir Walter Raleigh and that cloak episode. Miss Dolly nestled very cozily, en route, with a warm young arm flung carelessly over a broad masculine shoulder and her eyes were dreamy, the way heroines' eyes are in the books. She was not thinking of chimneys.

On the other side, she sat down, and imperiously—mistresses of slaves are always imperious—bade him take off her shoes. It was doubly exciting to vary the role of heroine with that of capricious slave-mistress. Of course, she might just as well have taken off her shoes on the other side and walked over but she never dreamed of doing that. After the slave had taken off her shoes, she herself removed her stockings, while the slave (seemingly cold and impassive as Angelo's marble Greek slave) looked away. Then she dabbled her tiny white feet in the cold stream. She was thinking of that Undine heroine. Dabbling her feet, also made her feel bookish. Only in the books the heroes (or slaves) gaze adoringly at said feet. Hers were worth gazing at, but Bob didn't seem to have eyes. Never mind! She told herself she liked that cold Anglo-Saxon phlegm (what an ugly word!) in a man. She saw in it a foil to her own temperamental disposition.

Having dabbled briefly, she held out a tiny foot and the slave dried it with his handkerchief, looking very handsome as he knelt before her. Then she put out the other and he repeated the operation. Then she put on her shoes and stockings. Then she remembered they had come ostensibly to fish and began whipping the stream spasmodically, while he did the same mechanically. They caught one or two speckled beauties, or Bob did. She couldn't land hers. They always got tangled in something which she thought very cute of them. She didn't feel annoyed at all when they got away, but just laughed as if it were the best kind of a joke, while Bob looked at her amazed. She called *that*"sport."

Then she made him build a "cunning little fire" on a rock and clean the fish and cook them and set them before her. She graciously let him sit by her side and partake of a few overdone titbits and a sandwich or two they had brought in the basket. But she also made him jump up every once in a while to do something, finding plenty of pretexts to keep him busy. In fact, she had never been more waited upon in her life, which was just what she wanted. Bob, however, didn't complain, for the minutes and hours went by and she asked no embarrassing questions. She didn't make herself disagreeable in that respect, and as long as she didn't, he didn't mind helping her over rocks, or toting her. At least, this was a respite. His headache wasn't quite so bad; the fresh air seemed to have helped it.

As for her thinking him one of those high-class society-burglars, or social buccaneers, it didn't so much matter to him, after all. He was getting rather accustomed to the idea. Of course, she would be terribly disappointed if she ever found out he wasn't one, but there didn't seem much chance of his ever clearing himself, in her mind, of that unjust suspicion. At least, he reflected moodily, he was capable of making one person in the world not positively miserable. Last night when he had parted from Dickie, he had found a small grain of the same kind of comfort, in the fact the he (or truth) had not harmed Dickie. But to-day Dickie had appeared saddened by Dan's and Clarence's troubles. Then, too, Bob had been obliged to walk off, right in front of Dickie's eyes with the temperamental young thing whom Dickie wanted to marry the worst way. And here he (Bob) was helping her over stones, "toting" frizzling trout for her, and performing a hundred other little services which should, by right, have been Dickie's pleasure and privilege to perform.

Bob murmured a few idle regrets about Dickie, but Miss Dolly dismissed them—and Dickie—peremptorily. She was sitting now, leaning against a tree and the slave, by command, was lying at her feet.

"Did you know," she said dreamily, "I am a new woman?"

He didn't know it. He never would have dreamed it, and he told her so.

"Yes," she observed, "I marched in the parade to Washington. That is, I started, went a mile or two, and then got tired. But I marched there, in principle, don't you see? I think women should throw off their shackles. Don't you?" Bob might have replied he didn't know that Miss Dolly ever had had any shackles to throw off, but she didn't give him time to reply. "I read a book the other day wherein the women do the proposing," she went on. "It's on an island and the women are 'superwomen.' All women are 'super' nowadays." She regarded him tentatively. Her glance was appraising. "Do you know of any reason why women should *not* do the proposing, Mr. Bennett?"

"Can't say that I do," answered Bob gloomily, feeling as if some one had suddenly laid a cold hand on his breast, right over where the heart is. Her words had caused his thoughts to fly back to another. She might not be proposing to the hammer-thrower at that moment in that "super" fashion, but the chances were that the hammer-thrower was proposing to her. He didn't look like a chap that would delay matters. He would strike while the iron was hot.

The temperamental young thing eyed Bob and then she eyed a dreamy-looking cloud. She let the fingers of one hand stray idly in Bob's hair as he lay with his head in the grass.

"It tries hard to curl, doesn't it?" she remarked irrelevantly.

"What?" said Bob absently, his mind about two miles and a half away.

"Your hair. You've got lovely hair." Bob looked disgusted. "It started to curl and then changed its mind, didn't it?" she giggled.

Bob muttered disagreeably.

"I suppose you were one of those curly-headed little boys?" went on the temperamental young thing.

"I don't know whether I was or not," he snapped. He was getting back into that snappy mood. Then it struck him this might not be quite the truth, the whole truth, and nothing but the truth, for he added sulkily; "Maybe I was."

"I can just see you," said the temperamental young thing in a far-off voice. "Nursie must have thought you a darling."

The slave again muttered ominously. He wished the temperamental little thing would take her fingers away. They trailed now idly over an ear.

"You're tickling," said Bob ill-naturedly.

She stopped trailing and patted instead—very gently and carelessly—as if she were patting a big Newfoundland dog which she owned all by herself. That pat expressed a sense of ownership.

"I'm wondering," she said, "whether it would make things nicer, if I did propose and we became engaged?"

"Oh," said Bob satirically, "you're wondering that, are you?"

"Yes." More tentative pats.

"And what do you suppose I'd say?" he demanded. He was feeling more and more grouchy all the time. He didn't want any of that "superwoman" business. He had already had one proposal. What mockery! A proposal! He heard again that other "Will you marry me?" and looked once more, in fancy, into the starry, enigmatical violet eyes. He experienced anew that surging sensation in his veins. And he awoke again to the hollow jest of those words! He felt, indeed, a moderately vivid duplication of all his emotions of the night before. The temperamental young thing's voice recalled him from the poignant recollections of the painful past into the dreary and monotonous present.

"Why, you actually blushed, just now," she said accusingly.

"Did I?" growled Bob, looking grudgingly into dark eyes where a moment before, in imagination, there had been starry violet ones.

"Yes, you did. And"—her voice taking a tenderer accent—"it was becoming, too."

"Rush of blood to the head," he retorted shortly. "Comes from lying like this."

"What would you say if I did?" she demanded, reverting to that other topic. "Propose, I mean? Would you accept? Would you take me— I mean, shyly suffer me," with a giggle, "to take you into my arms?"

"Quit joshing!" growled Bob.

"Answer. Would you?"

"No."

"No?" Bending over him more closely. For a "super," she was certainly wonderfully attractive in her slim young way at that moment. Not many of the inferior sex would have acted quite so stonily as Bob acted. He didn't show any more emotion when she bent over than one of those prostrate stone Pharaohs, or Rameses, which lie around with immovable features on the sands of Egypt. "You see you couldn't help it," the super-temperamental young thing assured him, confidentially.

"Ouch!" said Bob, for she was tickling again. He wished she would keep those trailing fingers in her lap. They felt like a fly perambulating his brow or walking around his ear.

"You'd just have to accept me," she added.

"Oh, you mean on account of that silly burglar business?"

"Of course. You left two or three thumb-prints in the room."

"I did?" That *was* incriminating. No getting around thumb-prints! He felt as if the temperamental little thing was weaving a mesh around him. In addition to being a "super," she was a Lady of Shalott.

Dolly thrilled with a sense of her power. She could play with poor Bob as a cat with a mouse; she could let him go so far and then put out her claws and draw him back.

"Besides, I found out you didn't quite tell me the truth about those accomplices of yours," she went on triumphantly. "You said there weren't any, and when I went out and looked around where the dog barked, I found footprints. They led to the trellis, right up into your room. The trellis, too, showed some person, or persons, had climbed up, for some of the boughs were broken. Deny now, if you can, you had visitors last night," she challenged him.

Bob didn't deny; he lay there helpless.

"Of course," she said with another giggle, "I might let you say you'll think it over. I might not press you too hard at once for an answer. I don't want you to reply: 'This is so sudden,' or anything like that." She got up suddenly with a little delirious laugh. "But I simply can't wait. You look so handsome when you're cross. Besides, it will be so exciting to be engaged to a—a—"

"Society-burglar—" grimly.

"That's it. I've never been engaged to a burglar before!"

"But you have been engaged?"

"Oh, yes. Lots of times. But not like this. This feels as if it might lead—"

"To the altar?" Satirically.

"Yes."

"But suppose I got caught?—that is, if I really enjoyed the distinction of being a burglar which I am not?"

"Then, of course, I never knew—you deceived me—poor innocent!—as well as the rest of the world. And there would be columns and columns in the papers. And some people would pity me, but most people would envy me. And I'd visit you in jail with a handkerchief to my eyes and be snap-shotted that way. And I'd sit in a dark corner in the court, looking pale and interesting. And the lady reporters would interview me and they'd publish my picture with yours—'Handsome Bob, the swell society yeggman. Member of one of the oldest families, etc.' And—and—"

"Great Scott!" cried Bob. She had that publicity-bee worse than Gee-gee. In another moment she'd be setting the day. "Shall we—ah!—retrace our steps?"

It was getting late. The hours had gone by somehow and as she offered no objections, they "retraced." For some time now she was silent. Perhaps she was imagining herself too happy for words. Once or twice she cast a sidelong glance shyly at Bob. It was the look of a capricious slave-owner metamorphosed, through the power of love, into a yielding and dependent young maiden. Bob was supposed to be the brutal conqueror. Meanwhile that young man strode along unheedingly. He didn't mind any little branches or bushes that happened to stand in his way and plowed right through them. It would have been the same, if he had met that historic bramble bush. A thousand scratches, more or less, wouldn't count.

"You can put your arm around me now," she observed, with another musical but detestable giggle, as they passed through a grove, not very far from the house. "It is quite customary here, you know."

He didn't know, but he obeyed. What else could he do?

"Now say something." Her voice had once more that ownership accent.

"What do you want me to say?" None too graciously.

"The usual thing! Those three words that make the world go around."

"But I don't." Even a worm will turn.

"You will." Softly.

"I won't."

"Oh, yes, you will." More softly. Then with a sigh: "This is the place. Under this oak, carved all over with hearts and things. Do it."

"What?" He looked down on lips red as cherries.

"Are you going to?"

"And if I don't?" he challenged her.

"Finger-prints!" she said. "Footmarks!"

"Oh, well! Confound it." And he did—the way a bird pecks at a cherry.

She straightened with another giggle. "Our first!" she said.

"Hope you're satisfied," he remarked grudgingly.

"It will do for a beginning. Oh, dear! some one saw us!" He looked around with a start, his unresponsive arm slipping from about a pliant waist.

"I don't see any one."

"He's dodged behind a tree. I think it was Dickie. And—yes, there are one or two other men. They—they seem to be dodging, too." Bob saw them now. One, he was sure, was the commodore.

"Funny performance, isn't it?" he said, with a sickly smile.

"Perhaps—?" She looked at him with genuine awe in the temperamental eyes. He read her thought; she thought—believed they had "come for him." She appeared positively startled, and—yes, sedulous! Maybe, she was discovering in herself a little bit of that "really, truly" feeling.

"Oh!" she said. "They mustn't—"

"Don't you worry," he reassured her. "I think I can safely promise you they won't do what you expect them to."

"You mean," joyously, "you have a way to circumvent them?" She was sure now he had; the aristocratic burglars always have. He would probably have a long and varied career before him yet.

"I mean just what I say. But I think they want to talk with me? Indeed, I'm quite sure they do. They are coming up now. Perhaps you'd better leave me to deal with them."

"You—you are sure they have no evidence to—?"

"Land me in jail? Positively. I assure you, on my honor, you are the only living person who, by any stretch of the imagination, could offer damaging testimony against me, along that line."

He spoke so confidently she felt it was the truth. "I believe you," she said. She wanted to say more, befitting the thrill of the moment, but she had no time. Dickie and two others were approaching. It might be best if he met them alone. So she slipped away and walked toward the house. It would be quite exciting enough afterward, she told herself, to find out what happened. It wasn't until she got almost to the house, that she remembered she ought to have asked Bob for a ring. Of course, he would have a goodly supply of them. Would it make her *particeps criminis* though, if she wore one of his rings? Then she concluded it wouldn't, because she was innocent of intention. She didn't know. She wondered, also, if she should announce her "engagement" right off, or wait a day or two. She decided to wait a day or two. But she told Miss Gwendoline Gerald what a lovely time she and Mr. Bennett had had together, fishing. And Miss Gerald smiled a cryptic smile.

Meanwhile Bob had met Dan and Dickie and Clarence.

CHAPTER XII—JUST ONE THING AFTER ANOTHER

It was far from a pleasant meeting. Dickie looked about as amiable as a wind or thunder demon, in front of a Japanese temple. That oscillatory performance beneath the "kissing-oak," as the noble tree was called, had been almost too much for Dickie. He seemed to have trouble in articulating.

"You're a nice one, aren't you?" he managed at length to say, and his tones were like the splutter of a defective motor. "You ought to be given a leather medal."

"Could I help it?" said Bob wearily. And then because he was too much of a gentleman to vouchsafe information incriminating a lady: "Usual place! Customary thing! Blame it on the oak! Ha! ha!" This wasn't evading the truth; it was simply facetiousness. Might as well meet this trio of dodging brigands with a smiling face! Dickie's vocal motor failed to explode, even spasmodically; that reply seemed to have extinguished him. But the commodore awoke to vivacity.

"Let us try to meet this situation calmly," he said, red as a turkey-cock. "But let us walk as we talk," taking Bob's arm and leading that young man unresistingly down a path to the driveway to the village. "I shouldn't by any chance want to encounter Mrs. Dan just yet," he explained. "So if you don't mind, we'll get away from here, while I explain."

Bob didn't mind. He saw no guile in the commodore's manner or words. Nor did he observe how Clarence looked at Dickie. The twilight shadows were beginning to fall.

"Briefly," went on the commodore, as he steered them out of the woods, "our worst fears have been realized. Negotiations with Gee-gee are in progress. Divorce papers will probably follow." Clarence on the other side of Dickie made a sound. "All this is your work." The commodore seemed about to become savage, but he restrained himself. "No use speaking about that. Also, it is too late for us to call the wager off and pay up. Mischief's done now."

"Why not make a clean breast of everything?" suggested Bob. "Say it was a wager, and—"

"A truth-telling stunt? That *would* help a lot." Contemptuously.

Dickie muttered: "Bonehead!"

"I mean, you can say there wasn't any harm," said Bob desperately. "That it was all open and innocent!"

"Much good my saying that would do!" snorted Dan. "You don't know Mrs. Dan."

"Or Mrs. Clarence," said Clarence weakly.

Bob hung his head.

"We've thought of one little expedient that may help," observed Dan, still speaking with difficulty. "While such influences as we could summon are at work on the New York end, we've got to square matters here. We've got to account for your—your—" here the commodore nearly choked—"extraordinary revelations."

"But how," said Bob patiently, "can you 'account' for them? I suppose you mean to make me out a liar?"

"Exactly," from the commodore coolly.

"I don't mind," returned Bob wearily, "as long as it will help you out and I'm not one. Only *I* can't say those things aren't true."

"You don't have to," said Dan succinctly. "There's an easier way than that. No one would believe you, anyway, now."

"That's true." Gloomily.

"All we need," went on Dan, brightening a bit, "is your cooperation."

"What can I do?"

"You don't do anything. We do what is to be done. You just come along."

"We take you into custody," interposed Clarence.

"Lock you up!" exploded Dickie once more. "And a good job."

"Lock me up?" Bob gazed at them, bewildered. Had the temperamental little thing "peached," after all? Impossible! And yet if she hadn't, how could Dan and Dickie and Clarence know he was a burglar—or rather, that a combination of unlucky circumstances made him seem one? Perhaps that kiss was a signal for them to step forward and take him. History was full of such kisses. And yet he would have sworn she was not that kind.

"You're to come along without making a fuss," said the commodore significantly.

"But I don't want to come along. This is going too far," remonstrated Bob. "I've a decided objection to being locked up as a burglar."

"Burglar!" exclaimed Dan.

"Don't know how you found out! Appearances may be against me, but," stopping in the road, "if you want me to go along, you've got to make me."

The trio looked at one another. "Maybe, he really is—" suggested Dickie, touching his forehead.

"Too much truth!" said Clarence with a sneer. "Feel half that way, myself!"

"Would be all the better for us, if it were really so," observed Dan. And to Bob: "You think that we think you're a burglar?"

"Don't you? Didn't you say something about locking me up?"

"But not in a jail."

Bob stared. "What then?"

"A sanatorium."

"Sanatorium?"

"For the insane."

"You mean—?"

"You're crazy," said Dan. "That's the ticket. Dickie found out, up at Mrs. Ralston's."

"Oh, Dickie did?" said Bob, looking at that young gentleman with lowering brows.

"You bet I did," returned Dickie. "I put in a good day," viciously, "while you were fishing."

"Yes," corroborated the commodore, "Dickie found a dozen people who think you're dottie on the crumpet, all right."

Bob folded his arms, still regarding Dickie. "You know what I've a mind to do to you?"

"Hold on!" said Dan hastily. "This matter's got to be handled tactfully. We can't, any one of us, give way to our personal feelings, however much we may want to. Let's be businesslike. Eh, Clarence? Businesslike."

"Sure," said Clarence faintly.

But Dickie, standing behind the commodore and Clarence, said something about tact being a waste of time in some cases. He said it in such a sneering nasty way that Bob breathed deep.

"I've simply got to spank that little rooster," he muttered.

But again the commodore smoothed things over. "Shut up, Dickie," he said angrily. "You'll spoil all. I'm sure Bob wants to help us out, if he can. He knows it's really up to him, to do so. Bob's a good sport." It was an awful effort for the commodore to appear nice and amiable, but he managed to, for the moment. "You will help us out, won't you?" he added, placing velvety fingers on Bob's arm.

But Bob with a vigorous swing shook off those fingers. He didn't intend being taken into custody. Dan and the others might as well understand that, first as last. The commodore's voice grew more appealing.

"Don't you see you're being crazy will account for everything?"

"Oh, will it?" In a still small voice.

"Miss Gwendoline asked me if you'd showed signs before coming down here?" piped up Dickie. And again Bob breathed deep. Then his thoughts floated away. Dickie was too insignificant to bother with.

"Hallucinations!" observed the commodore briskly. "Fits you to a T!"

Bob didn't answer. He was trying to think if *she*—Miss Gwendoline—hadn't said something about hallucinations?

"You simply imagined all those things you confided to Mrs. Dan. You didn't mean to tell what wasn't so, but you couldn't help yourself. You really believed it all, at the time. You are irresponsible."

"Maybe you'll tell me next there isn't any Gee-gee," said Bob. "Also, that Miss Gid-up is but an empty coinage of the brain?"

"No, we'll do better than that. The existence of a Gee-gee accounts, in part, for your condition. First stage, Gee-gee on the brain; then, brain-storm! Gee-gee is part of your obsession!"

"You talk, think and dream of Gee-gee," interposed Clarence. "We've got it all doped out. You are madly jealous. You imagine every man is in love with her. You even attribute to Dan here, ulterior motives."

"I mentioned to Miss Gerald, privately, that a certain very fascinating but nameless young show-girl might be your trouble," said Dickie.

Again Bob did a few deep-breathing exercises, and again he managed to conquer himself.

"Don't you see we've simply got to lock you up?" said the commodore. "You're a menace to the community; you're a happy home-breaker. You may do something desperate."

"I might," said Bob, looking the commodore in the eye.

Dan overlooked any covert meaning. "We take your case in time," he went on. "You go into an institution, stay a week, or two—or shall we say, three," insinuatingly, "and you come out cured."

"Wouldn't that be nice?" said Bob. They were going to put truth in a crazy-house. That's what it amounted to. "But how about Gid-up? Did I have an obsession about her, too?"

"Oh, as Gee-gee's chum she is part of the brainstorm and that drags poor old Clarence in,—Clarence who is as ignorant of the existence of Gid-up as I am of Gee-gee."

"And that's the truth," said Clarence stoutly.

Bob laughed. He couldn't help it. Perhaps many of the people in jails and crazy-houses were only poor misguided mortals who had gone wrong looking for truth. Maybe some of them had met with that other kind of truth (Dan's kind and Clarence's kind) and they hadn't the proper vision to see it was the truth (that is, the world's truth).

"Got it fixed all right," went on the commodore. "Doc, up there at the house, has written a letter to the head of an eminently respectable institution, for eminently respectable private patients. It's not far away and the head is a friend of Doc's. Dickie saw to the details. It's a good place. Kind gentle attendants; nourishing food. Isn't that what the Doc said, Dickie?"

"I guess the food won't hurt *him*" said Dickie, regarding Bob. Maybe, Dickie wouldn't have minded if Bob had had an attack, or two, of indigestion.

"Doc says they're especially humane to the violent," continued the commodore, unmindful of Bob's ominous silence. It seemed as if Dan was talking to gain time, for he looked around where the bushes cast dark shadows, as if to locate some spot. "None of that slugging or straight-jacket business! Doc talked it over with the judge and some of the others. Judge said he'd committed a lot of people who hadn't acted half as crazy as you have. You see Dickie had to take him into his confidence a little bit and the Doc, too. Doc diagnosed your breakdown as caused by drugs and alcohol."

"So you made me out a dipsomaniac?" observed Bob.

"What else was there to do? Didn't you bring it on yourself?"

Dan now stopped, not far from a clump of bushes. Down the road stood a stalled motor-car vaguely distinguishable in the dusk. Its occupant, or occupants had apparently gone to telephone for help.

"You bet I made you out a 'dippy,'" said Dickie with much satisfaction.

A white light shone from Bob's eyes. Then he shrugged his broad shoulders.

"Good night," he said curtly and turned to go.

But at that instant the commodore emitted a low whistle and two men sprang out of the bushes. At the same moment the trio precipitated themselves, also, on Bob. It was a large load. He "landed" one or two on somebody and got one or two in return himself. Dickie rather forgot himself in the excitement of the moment and was unnecessarily forceful, considering the odds. But Bob was big and husky and for a little while he kept them all busy. His football training came in handy. Numbers, however, finally prevailed, and though he heaved and struggled, he had to go down. Then they sat on him, distributing themselves variously over his anatomy.

"Thought I was giving you that charming little chat, just for the pleasure of your company, did you?" panted the commodore, from somewhere about the upper part of Bob? "Why, I was just leading you here."

"And he came like a lamb!" said Clarence, holding an arm.

"Or a big boob!" from Dickie, who had charge of a leg.

Bob gave a kick and it caught Dickie. The little man went bowling down the road like a ten-pin. But after that, there wasn't much kick left in Bob. They tied him tight and bore him (or truth, trussed like a fowl), to the car. Some of them got in to keep him company. There wasn't anything the matter with the car. It could speed up to about sixty, or seventy, at a pinch. It went "like sixty" now.

"If he tries to raise a hullabaloo, toot your horn," said the commodore, when he got his breath, to the driver. "At the same time I'll wave my hat and act like a cut-up. Then they'll only take us for a party of fuzzled joy-riders."

"I don't think he'll make much noise now," shouted Dickie significantly, from behind. "We'll jolly well see to that."

"How long will it take you to make the bug-house?" the commodore asked the man at the wheel.

"We should reach the private sanatorium in less than an hour," answered that individual.

CHAPTER XIII—AN ENFORCED REST CURE

They kept him two days in the padded room on Dickie's recommendation, who made Bob out as highly dangerous. "Powerful and vicious," he described him to the suave individual in charge of the "sanatorium." That particular apartment was somewhat remote from the other rooms, so that any noises made by the inmate of the former wouldn't disturb the others. Becoming more reconciled to the inevitable, Bob found the quiet of the padded room rather soothing to his shaken nerves. He didn't have to talk to hardly a soul. Only an attendant came around once in a while to shove cautiously something edible at him, but the attendant didn't ask any questions and Bob didn't have to tell him any truths. It was a joyful relief not to have to tell truths.

Bob's eye was swollen and he had a few bruises, but they didn't count. He had observed with satisfaction that Dickie's lip had an abrasion and that one of his front teeth seemed missing. Dickie would have to wait until nature and art had repaired his appearance before he could once more a-wooing go. Bob didn't want the temperamental young thing himself, but he couldn't conscientiously wish Dickie success in that quarter, after the unnecessarily rough and unsportsmanlike manner in which Dickie had comported himself against him (Bob).

At first, it had occurred to Bob to take the attendant—and through him, the manager of the institution—into his confidence, but for two reasons he changed his mind about doing so. The attendant would probably receive Bob's confidence as so many illusions; he would smile and say "Yes—quite so!" or "There! there!"—meaning Bob would get over said illusions some day, and that was why he was there. He was being treated for them. Again, if he unbosomed himself fully, as to the fundamental cause of all this trouble and turmoil, he would lose to the commodore, et al., and have to pay that note which he didn't very well see how he could pay.

Bob gritted his teeth. Would it not be better to win now to spite them and in spite of everything? About the worst that could happen, had happened. Why not accept, then, this enforced sojourn philosophically and when the time came, he would walk up to the captain's (or commodore's) office and demand a little pay-envelope as his hard-earned wage? There would be a slight balm in that pay-envelope. With the contents thereof, he could relieve some of dad's necessities which soon would be pressing. Why not, with a little stretch of the imagination, tell himself he (Bob) was only taking a rest cure? People paid big prices for a fashionable rest cure. They probably charged pretty stiff prices here, but it wouldn't cost him a cent. His dear friends who put him here would have to pay. He wasn't a voluntary boarder. They would have to vouch for him and his bills. So Bob made up his mind to have as good a time as he could; in other words, to grin and bear it, as best he might.

It was a novel experience. Maybe he might write an article about it for one of the Sunday newspapers some day—"How It Feels for a Sane Person to be Forcibly Detained in an Insane Asylum, by One who Has Been There." The editor could put all manner of gay and giddy head-lines over such an experience. Bob tried to chronicle his feelings in the padded cell, but he couldn't conjure up anything awful or harrowing. There weren't spiders, or rats, or any crawly things to lend picturesqueness to the situation. It was only deadly quiet—the kind of quiet he needed.

He slept most of those first two days, making up for hours of lost sleep. His swollen eye became less painful and his appetite grew large and normal. He had to eat with his fingers because they were afraid to trust him with a knife and fork, but he told himself cheerfully that high-class Arabs still ate that way, and that all he had to do was to sit cross-legged, to be strictly *comme il faut*—that is, from the Arab's standpoint. Since he had adopted truth as his mentor, Bob had learned, however, that "what should be" or "what shouldn't," or "mustn't," depends a great deal upon the standpoint, and he was beginning to be very suspicious, or critical, about the standpoint.

The third day the doctor in charge thought he could trust him in a room without pads. Bob had a good color, his eye was clear and his appearance generally reassuring, so they gave him now the cutest little cubby-hole, with a cunning little bed and a dear little window, with flowers outside and iron bars between the inmate and the flowers. The managing-medico proudly called Bob's attention to the flowers and the view. One gazing out could see miles and miles of beautiful country. The managing-med. talked so much about that view that Bob chimed in and said it was lovely, too, only, it reminded him of the bone set just beyond reach of a dog chained to *his* cute little cubby-hole; or the jug of water and choice viands the Bedouins of the desert set before their victim after they have buried him to the neck in the sand. Bob was going on, trying to think of other felicitous comparisons, when he caught a look in the managing-med's. eye that stopped him.

"I wonder if you are well enough, after all, to appreciate this cozy and home-like little apartment?" said the med. musingly.

Bob hastily apologized for the figures of speech. The padded place was very restful, no doubt, but he was quite rested now. Any more padded-room kind of rest would be too much. He looked at the view and expatiated upon it, even calling attention to certain charming details of the landscape. The flowers made a charming touch of color and they were just the kind of flowers he liked—good, old-fashioned geraniums! He could say all this and still tell the truth. The medico studied him attentively; then he concluded he would risk it and permit Bob to stay in the room.

But he didn't stay there long. Several nights later a pebble clicked against his window; at first, he did not notice. The sound was repeated. Then Bob got up, went to his window, raised it noiselessly and looked out. In the shadow, beneath the window, stood a figure.

"Catch," whispered a voice and instinctively Bob put out his hand. But he didn't catch; he missed. Again and again some one below tossed something until finally he did catch. He looked at the object—a spool of thread. Now what on earth did he want with a spool of thread? Did the person below think some of his garments needed mending? It was strong, serviceable enough thread.

For some moments Bob cogitated, then going to the bureau, he picked up a tooth-brush, tied it to the thread, and let it down. After an interval he pulled up the thread; the tooth-brush had disappeared and a file was there in its stead. Then Bob tied to the thread something else and instead of it, he got back the end of an excellent manila rope. After that he went to work. It took Bob about an hour to get those bars out; it took him, then, about a minute to get out himself. Fortunately some one in a near-by room was having a tantrum and the little rasping sound of the filing couldn't be heard. The louder the person yelled, the harder Bob filed.

When he reached the earth some one extended a hand and led him silently out of the garden and into the road beyond. Bob went along meekly and obediently. Not far down the road was a taxicab. Bob got in and his fair rescuer followed. So far he hadn't said a word to her; language seemed superfluous. But as they dashed away, she murmured:

"Isn't it lovely?""

"Is it?" he asked. Somehow he wasn't feeling particularly jubilant over his escape. In fact, he found himself wondering almost as soon as he had reached the earth, if it wouldn't have been wiser, after all, to have spent the rest of those three weeks in pleasant seclusion. The presence of the temperamental young thing suggested new and more perplexing problems perhaps. He had regarded her as somewhat of a joke, but she wasn't a joke just now; she was a reality. What was he going to do with her, and with himself, for that matter? Why were they dashing madly across the country like that together?

It was as if he were carrying her off, and he certainly didn't want to do that. He wasn't in love with her, and she wasn't with him. At least, he didn't think she was. It was only her temperamental disposition that caused her to imagine she was in love, because she thought him something that he wasn't. And when she found out he wasn't, but was only a plain, ordinary young man, not of much account anyhow, what a shock would be the awakening! Perhaps he'd better stop the machine, go back into the garden, climb up to his room in the crazy-house and tumble into bed? His being here, embarked on a preposterous journey, seemed a case of leaping before looking, or thinking.

"Why so quiet, darling?" giggled the temperamental young thing, snuggling closer.

"Don't call me that. I—I won't stand it."

"All right, dearie." With another giggle.

"And drop that 'dearie' dope, too," he commanded.

"Just as you say. Only what *shall* I call you?"

"I guess plain 'darn fool' will do."

"Oh, you're too clever to be called that," she expostulated.

"Me, clever?" Scornfully.

"Yes; think how long you have fooled the police."

"I wish you wouldn't talk such nonsense." Irritably.

"I won't. On condition!"

"What?"

"If you'll put your arm around me."

"I won't."

"Oh, yes, you will." She adjusted it for him.

"All right! If you want some one to hug you when he doesn't want to!" he said in aggrieved tones.

"That makes it all the nicer," she returned. "There are ever so many men that want to. This—this is so different!" With a sigh.

"There you go, with some more nonsense talk!" grumbled Bob.

"Well," she giggled, "there's always a way to make a poor, weak, helpless little thing stop talking."

"Of all the assurance!" he gasped.

"I love to have some one I can command to make love to me."

"I'm going back." Disgustedly.

"Oh, no, you're not. You can't."

"Why?"

"You'd be arrested, if you did. They are coming for you. That's why I came—to circumvent them!"

"They?"

"All has been discovered."

"I fail to understand."

"What did you do with it?" she countered.

"It?"

"The swag."

Bob started to withdraw his arm but she clapped a small warm hand on his big warm hand and held his strong right arm about her slim, adaptable waist. Her head trailed on his shoulder, while she started floating off in dreamland.

"I just love eloping," she murmured.

"What was that last word?" he observed combatively.

"Elope! elope! elope!" she whispered dreamily, her slim, young feminine figure close to his big masculine bulk.

"So you think you're eloping with me?" said Bob ominously.

"I know I am." In that musical die-away tone. "We're headed straight for old New York and we're going to get married in the little church around the corner. Then"—with a happy laugh—"we may have to disguise ourselves and flee."

"May I kindly inquire—that is, if I have any voice in our future operations—*why* we may have to disguise ourselves?"

"In case they should want to capture you. The police, I mean."

"Police?" he said.

"Didn't I just tell you they were coming for you?"

"Indeed?" He looked down in her eyes to see if she was in earnest. He believed she was. "For what?"

"Oh, you know." She raised her lips. "Say, that was a real stingy one, under the oak."

"You say all has been discovered?" went on Bob, disregarding her last remark.

"I say that was a real stingy—"

"Hang it!" But he had to. He knew he had to get that idea out of her head, before he could get any more real information from her.

"And think how you deceived poor little me, about it!" she purred contentedly. After all, thought Bob, it didn't take "much of a one" to satisfy her. She had only wanted "it," perhaps, because "it" fitted in; "it" went with eloping. Perhaps "it" would have to happen about once so often. Bob hoped not. She was a dainty little tyrant who let him see plainly she had sharp claws. She could scratch as well as purr. Somehow, he felt that he was doubly in her power—that he was doubly her slave now—that something had happened which made him so. He could not imagine what it was.

"They're keeping it very quiet, though," she went on. "The robbery, I mean!"

"There has been a robbery at Mrs. Ralston's?"

"Of course. And you didn't know a thing about it?" she mocked him.

"I certainly did not."

"You say that just as if it were so," she observed admiringly. "I don't suppose you are aware that some one did really substitute a counterfeit brooch for Mrs. Vanderpool's wonderful pink pearl and bronze diamond brooch, after all? Oh, no, you don't know that.

You're only a poor little ignorant dear. Bless its innocent little heart! It didn't know a thing. Not it!" She was talking baby-talk now, the while her fingers were playing with Bob's ear. He was so interested in what she was saying, however, that he failed to note the baby-talk and overlooked the liberties she was taking with his hearing apparatus.

"By jove!" he exclaimed. "That accounts for what I thought I saw in the hall that night when I left your room. Imagined I saw some one! Believe now it was some one, after all. And that door I heard click? Whose door is that on the other side of the hall from your room and about twenty-five feet nearer the landing?" Excitedly.

"Gwendoline Gerald's," was the unexpected answer.

Bob caught his breath. He was becoming bewildered. "But nothing was missing from Miss Gerald's room, was there?" he asked.

"Don't *you* know?" said she.

"I do not."

"My! aren't you the beautiful fibber! I'm wondering if you ever tell the truth?"

"I don't tell anything else." Indignantly. "And that's the trouble."

"And how well you stick to it!" Admiringly. "If you tell such ones *before*, how will it be *after*?"

"After what?" he demanded.

"The church ceremony," she giggled.

"Don't you worry about that. There isn't going to be any."

"It's perfectly lovely of you to say there isn't. It will be such fun to see you change your mind." She spoke in that regular on-to-Washington tone. "I can just see you walking up the aisle. Won't you look handsome? And poor, demure little me! I shan't look like hardly anything."

Bob pretended not to hear.

"You say they are keeping it very quiet about the robbery at the Ralston house. How, then, did you come to know?"

"Eavesdropping." Shamelessly. "Thought it was necessary you should know the 'lay of the land.' But never mind the 'how.' It is sufficient that I managed to overhear Lord Stanfield say he was going to send for you. Gwendoline Gerald knows about the robbery and so does her aunt and Lord Stanfield, but it's being kept from all the other guests for the present. Even Mrs. Vanderpool doesn't know. She still thinks the brooch she is wearing is the real one, poor dear! Lord Stanfield discovered it wasn't. He asked her one day to let him see it. Then, he just said: 'Aw! How interesting!'—that is, to her. But to Mrs. Ralston he said it was an imitation and that some guest had substituted the false brooch for the real. Mrs. Vanderpool is not to know because Lord Stanfield says the thief must not dream he is suspected. He wants to give him full swing yet a while— 'enough rope to hang himself with,' were the words he used. It seems Lord Stanfield anticipated things would be missing. He said he knew when a certain person—he didn't say whom"—gazing up at Bob adoringly—"appeared on the scene, things just went. That's why Lord Stanfield got asked to the Ralston house. Then when he said he was coming after you, I thought it would be such a joke if you weren't there to receive him. And that's why I came to elope with you. And isn't it all too romantic for anything? I am sure none of those plays comes up to it. Maybe you'll dramatize our little romance some day—that is—"

Miss Dolly suddenly stopped. "Isn't that a car coming up behind?"

Bob looked around, too, and in the far distance saw a light. "Believe it is," he answered.

She leaned forward and spoke to the driver. They were traveling with only one lamp lighted; the driver now put that out. Then he went on until he came to a private roadway, leading into some one's estate, when quickly turning, he ran along a short distance and finally stopped the car in a dark shaded spot. Bob gazed back and in a short time saw a big car whir by. Idly he wondered whether it contained the police, or the managing medico and some of his staff. Between them, he was promised a right lively time—altogether too lively. He wondered which ones would get him first? It was a kind of a competition and he would be first prize to the winners. Well, it was well to have the enemy—or half of the enemy—in front of him. Of course, the other half might come up any moment behind. He would have to take that chance, he thought, as they now returned to the highway. Meanwhile Miss Dolly's eyes were bright with excitement. She was enjoying herself very much.

CHAPTER XIV—MUTINY

They resumed the conversation where they had left off.

"It seems to me," said Bob, "from all you say, that monocle-man has been a mighty busy person."

"Of course you knew right along what he is. You didn't need any information from poor little me about him. He couldn't fool great big You!" she affirmed admiringly.

"I can imagine what he is—now," observed Bob meditatively. He was turning over in his mind what she had said about that substituted brooch. The some one Bob had imagined he had seen in the hall, after leaving Miss Dolly's room, might not have been the real thief, after all; it might have been the monocle-man on the lookout for the thief. And perhaps the monocle-man had seen Bob. That was the reason he was "coming for him." Bob could imagine dear old dad's feelings, if he (Bob) got sent to Sing Sing. What if, instead of rustling and rising to the occasion, in that fine, old honorable Japanese way, Bob should bring irretrievable disgrace on an eminently respectable family name?

He could see himself in stripes now, with his head shaved, and doing the lock-step. Perhaps, even at that moment, descriptions of him were being sent broadcast. And if so, it would look as if he were running away from the officers of the law, which would be tantamount to a confession of guilt. Bob shivered. The temperamental young thing did not share his apprehensions.

"Of course, Lord Stanfield only *thinks* he has evidence enough to convict you," she said confidently. "But you'll meet him at every point and turn the laugh on him."

"Oh, will I?" said Bob ironically.

"And you'll make him feel so cheap! Of course, you've got something up your sleeve—"

"Wish I had," he muttered.

"Something deep and mysterious," she went on in that confident tone. "That's why you acted so queer toward some people. You had a purpose. It was a ruse. Wasn't it now?" she concluded triumphantly.

"It was not." Gruffly.

"Fibber! every time you fib, you've got to—" She put up her lips.

"This is getting monotonous," grumbled Bob.

"On the contrary!" breathed the temperamental young thing. "I find it lovely. Maybe you'll learn how sometime."

"Don't want to," he snapped.

"Oh, yes, you do. But as I was saying, you got yourself put in that sanatorium to mislead everybody. It, too, was a ruse—a part of the game. It's all very clear—at least, to me!"

He stared at her. And she called *that* clear? "When did you leave Mrs. Ralston's?" he demanded.

"About three hours ago. Said I'd a headache and believed I'd go to my room. But I didn't. I just slipped down to the village and hired a taxi. Maybe we'd better keep our marriage a secret, at first." Irrelevantly.

"Maybe we had," answered Bob. And then he called out to the man in front. "Stop a moment."

Before Miss Dolly had time to expostulate, the driver obeyed. Bob sprang out.

"You aren't going to leave me, are you?" said the temperamental little thing. "If so—" She made as if to get out, too.

"No; I'm not going to leave you just yet," answered Bob. Then to the driver: "See here! Your blamed machine is turned in the wrong direction. You know where you're going to take us?"

"New York."

"No; back to Mrs. Ralston's. You take the first cross-road you come to and steer right for there."

"You're not to do any such thing," called out Miss Dolly. "You're to go where *I* tell you."

"You're to do nothing of the sort," said Bob. "You're to go where *I* tell you."

The driver scratched his head.

"Which is it to be?" asked Bob. "This is the place to have an understanding."

"The lady hired me," he answered.

"Yes, and I won't pay you at all, if you don't mind," said Miss Dolly in firm musical accents.

"Guess that settles it," observed the driver.

"You mean—?" began Bob, eying him.

"It means I obey orders. She's my 'fare,' not you. We just picked you up."

"And that's your last word?" Ominously.

"Say, lady"—the driver turned wearily—"have I got to suppress this crazy man you got out of the bughouse?"

"Maybe that would be a good plan," answered Miss Dolly, militancy now in her tone. "That is, if he doesn't get in, just sweet and quiet-like."

"It'll be twenty dollars extra," said the man, rising. He was a big fellow, too.

"Make it thirty," returned Miss Dolly spiritedly. It was an issue and had to be met. There was an accent of "On-to-Parliament!" in her voice. One can't show too much mercy to a "slave" when he revolts. One has to suppress him. One has to teach him who is mistress. A stern lesson, and the slave learns and knows his place.

"Now mind the lady and get back where you belong," said the driver roughly to Bob. "Your tiles are loose, and the lady knows what is good for a dingbat like you." Possibly he thought the display of a little authority would be quite sufficient to intimidate a recent "patient." They usually became quite mild, he had heard, when the keepers talked right up to them, like that. The effect of his language and attitude upon Bob was not, however, quieting; something seemed to explode in his brain and he made one spring and got a football hold; then he heaved and the big man shot over his shoulder as if propelled from a catapult. He came down in a ditch, where the breath seemed to be knocked out of him. Bob got on in front. As he started the machine, the man sat up and looked after him. He didn't try to get up though; he just looked. No doubt he had had the surprise of his life.

"I'll leave the car in the village when I'm through with it," Bob called back. "A little walk won't hurt you."

The man didn't answer. "Gee! but that's a powerful lunatic for a poor young lady to have on her hands!" he said to himself.

An hour or so later Bob drew up in front of Mrs. Ralston's house. He opened the door politely for Miss Dolly and the temperamental young thing sprang out. The guests were still up, indulging in one of those late dances that begin at the stroke of twelve, and the big house showed lights everywhere. There were numerous other taxis and cars in front and Bob's arrival attracted no particular attention. Miss Dolly gave him a look, militant, but still adoring. She let him see she had claws.

"Maybe I'll tell," she said.

"Go ahead," he answered.

"Aren't you afraid?"

"No." He hadn't done anything wrong.

"Aren't you even sorry?" she asked, lingering.

"For what?"

"Being so rough to that poor man?"

"I'm not. Good night."

"Good night—darling." She threw out that last word as a challenge. It had a tender but sibilant sound. It was a mixture of a caress and a scratch. It meant she hadn't given up her hold on him. He might have defeated her in one little contest, but she would weave new ways to entrap him. She might even manage to make him out a murderer—he had been so many things since embarking on that mercurial truth-telling career—and then she would give him the choice of the altar or the chair.

He started the machine and she watched him disappear, musingly. There was a steely light, too, in her eyes. He was a mutineer and mutineers should, figuratively, be made to walk the plank. Should she put him in jail and then come and weep penitently? At least, it would be thrilling. Certainly anything was better than that cast-off feeling. She felt no better than cast-off clothes. This great big brute of a handsome man, instead of jumping at the chance to elope with one who had everything to offer such a one as he, had just turned around and brought her back home.

Maybe he thought she wasn't worthy of him. Oh, wasn't she? Her small breast arose mutinously, while that cast-off sensation kept growing and growing. After rescuing him and saving him, instead of calling her "his beautiful doll" or other pet names, and humming glad songs to her—how they would "row, row, row" on some beautiful river of love—or stroll, stroll, stroll through pathways of perfume and bliss—instead of regaling her with these and other up-to-date expressions, appropriate to the occasion, he had repudiated her, cast her off, deposited her here on the front steps, unceremoniously, carelessly, indifferently.

Her cheeks burned at the affront. It was too humiliating. The little hands closed. The temperamental fingernails bit into the tender palms. At that moment the monocle-man sauntered out of the house and on to the veranda, near where Miss Dolly was standing. She turned to him quickly. Her temperament had about reached the Borgia pitch.

Bob went on down to the village and to the taxi stand near the station where he had promised to leave the machine. The last train had just passed by, after depositing the last of late-comers from the gay metropolis. Most of them looked fagged; a few were mildly "corned." Bob regarded them absently and then gave a violent start.

"Gee-gee!" he gasped.

There she was, in truth, the beauteous Gee-gee, and the fair Gid-up, too! Bob gazed in consternation from reddish hair to peroxide. The two carried grips and were dressed in their best—that is to say, each wore the last thing in hats and the final gasp in gowns.

"Guess none of those society dames will have a thing on us, when it comes to rags," Gid-up murmured to Gee-gee, as they crossed the platform with little teeny-weeny steps and headed toward a belated hack or two and Bob's machine. That young man yet sat on the driver's seat of the taxi; he was too paralyzed to move as he watched them approach. Where on earth were Gee-gee and Gid-up going? He feared to learn. He had an awful suspicion.

"Chauffeur!" Gee-gee raised a begloved finger as she hailed Bob. The glove had seen better days, but Gee-gee didn't bother much about gloves. When she had attained the finality in hats and the *ne plus ultra* in skirts, hosiery and stilts (you asked for "shoes") she hadn't much time, or cash, left for gloves which were always about the same old thing over and over again, anyway. "Chauffeur!" repeated Gee-gee.

"Meaning me?" inquired Bob in muffled tones. Why didn't she take a hack? He had drawn up his taxi toward the dark end of the platform.

"Yes, meaning you!" replied Gee-gee sharply. "Can't say I see any other human spark-plug in this one-night burg."

"What can I do for you?" stammered Bob. He was glad it was so shadowy where he sat, and he devoutly hoped he would escape recognition.

"What can he do? Did you hear that?" Gee-gee appealed indignantly to Gid-up. "I don't suppose a great jink like you knows enough to get down and take a lady's bag? Or, to open the door of the limousine?"

"Well, you see this machine's engaged," mumbled Bob. "No, I don't mean that." Hastily. "I mean I'm not the driver of this car. It doesn't belong to me. And that's the truth."

"Where is the driver?" Haughtily. "Send for him at once." Gee-gee did not like to be crossed. Gid-up was more good-natured; she only shifted her gum.

"I can't send for him," said Bob drawing his hat down farther over his face. "He's down the road."

"What's he doing there?"

"I don't know. Maybe, he's walking; maybe, he's sitting in the ditch."

Gee-gee stared, but she could see only a big shadowy form; she couldn't make out Bob's features. "The boob's got bees," she confided to Gid-up, and then more imperatively: "Are you going to get off your perch and let us in?"

"Beg to be excused," muttered Bob. "Hack over there! Quick! Before some one else gets it."

That started them away. The teeny-weeny steps encompassed, accelerando, the distance between Bob and his old friend, the hackman who had laughed at what he supposed were Bob's eccentricities. The hackman got down and hoisted in the grips.

"Where to?" he said.

Bob listened expectantly. He feared what was coming.

"Mrs. Ralston's," answered Gee-gee haughtily. At the same time Gid-up threw away her gum. She would have to practise being without it.

Bob drearily watched the hack roll away. He refused another offer of a fare—this time from a bibulous individual who had supped, not wisely, but too well—and nearly got into a fight because the bibulous individual was persistent and discursive. Then Bob walked away; he didn't think where he was going; he only wanted to get away from that chauffeur job. What would come of these new developments, he wondered? The temperamental young thing was "peeved," and the ponies (not equine) had come galloping into the scene at the critical moment.

He tried to account for their presence. Undoubtedly it was a coup of Mrs. Dan's. When she learned that dear Dan was bringing counter-influence to bear upon her witnesses, she arranged to remove them. She brought them right into her own camp. How? Gee-gee and Gid-up did a really clever and fairly refined musical and dancing act together. Mrs. Ralston frequently called upon professional talent to help her out in the entertaining line. It is true, Gee-gee and Gid-up were hardly "high enough up," or well enough known, to commend themselves ordinarily to the good hostess in search of the best and most expensive artists, but then Mrs. Dan may have brought influence to bear upon Mrs. Ralston. And Mrs. Clarence may have seconded Mrs. Dan's efforts. They may have said Gee-gee and Gid-up were dashing and different, and would be, at least, a change. They may have exaggerated the talents of the pair and pictured them as rising stars whom it would be a credit for Mrs. Ralston to discover. The hostess was extremely good-natured and liked to oblige her friends, or to comply with their requests.

Of course, the young ladies would not appear on the scene as Gee-gee and Gid-up, in all probability. No doubt, they would assume other and more appropriate cognomens (non equine). The last show they had played in, had just closed, so a little society engagement, with strong publicity possibilities, on the side, could not be anything but appealing, especially to Gee-gee with her practical tendencies.

Of course, they would have to make a brave effort to put on their society manners, but Gid-up had once had a home and Gee-gee knew how people talked in the society novels. Trust Gee-gee to adapt herself!

Bob felt he could figure it all out. Their coming so late would seem to indicate they had been sent for in haste. Mrs. Dan, perhaps, had become alarmed and wasn't going to take any more chances with the commodore who was capable of sequestering her witnesses, of inveigling them on board one of his friend's yachts, for example, and then marooning them on a desert isle, or transporting them to one of those cafe chantants of Paris. Besides, with that after-midnight "hug" and "grizzly" going on, Mrs. Dan knew it wouldn't much matter how late the pair arrived.

By the time Bob had argued this out, he was a long way from the village. He had been walking mechanically toward the Ralston house and now found himself on the verge of the grounds. After a moment's hesitation, he went in and walked up to the house. The dancing had, at length, ceased and the big edifice was now almost dark. The inmates, or most of them, seemed to have retired. A few of the men might yet be lingering in the smoking-room or over billiards. For a minute or two Bob stood in silent meditation. Then his glance swept toward a certain trellis, and a sudden thought smote him.

Wasn't he still Mrs. Ralston's guest? The period for which he had been invited hadn't expired and he hadn't, as yet, been asked to vacate the premises. True, some people had forcibly, and in a most highhanded manner, removed him for a brief period, but they had not been acting for Mrs. Ralston, or by her orders. He was, therefore, legitimately still a guest and it was obviously his duty not to waive the responsibility. He might not want to come back but he had to. That even-tenor-of-his-way condition demanded it. Besides, manhood revolted against retreat under fire. To run away, as he had told himself in the car with Miss Dolly, was a confession of guilt. He must face them once more—even Miss Gerald and the hammer-thrower. He could in fancy, see himself handcuffed in her presence, but he couldn't help it. Better that, than to be hunted in the byways and hovels of New York! Oddly, too, the idea of a big comfortable bed appealed to him.

He climbed up the trellis and stood on the balcony upon which his room opened. Pushing up a window, he entered and feeling around in the darkness he came upon his grip where he had left it. He drew the curtains, turned on the lights and undressed. He acted just as if nothing had happened. Then, donning his pajamas, he turned out the lights, drew back the curtains once more, and tumbled into the downy.

CHAPTER XV—AN EXTRAORDINARY INTERVIEW

But he could not sleep; his brain was too busy. He wondered in what part of the house Gee-gee and Gid-up were domiciled? He wondered if Mrs. Dan and Mrs. Clarence were drawing up affidavits? He wondered if that taxicab man had yet come to town and if he would get out a warrant, charging him (Bob) with assault? He wondered if Dan and Clarence knew Gee-gee and Gid-up were here, and if so, what would they do about it? Would they, too, come prancing on the scene? He wondered if Miss Gerald were engaged to the hammer-man? He wondered if the maniac-medico would think of looking for him (Bob) here? He wondered where the police were looking for him and who was the thief, anyway? This last mental query led him to consider the guests, one by one.

He began with the bishop. Suspicion, of course, could not point in that direction. Still, there was that play, *Deacon Brodie*—a very good man was a thief in it. But a deacon wasn't a bishop. Besides, Bob had great respect for the cloth. He dismissed the bishop with an inward apology. He next considered the judge, but the judge was too portly for those agile sleight-of-hand feats and the deft foot-work required. He passed on to the doctor. The doctor had delicate little hands, adapted for filching work, but he was too much absorbed in cutting up little dogs and cats to care for such insensible trifles as glittering gee-gaws. The doctor might be capable of absconding with a Fido or somebody's pet Meow, but an inanimate Kooh-i-nor would hold for him no temptations. So from Doc, Bob passed on to Mrs. Van. But she wouldn't surreptitiously appropriate her own brooch. He even considered the temperamental young thing whose interest in crime and criminals was really shocking.

He had got about this far in thrashing things over in his mind when a rather startling realization that he wasn't alone in the room smote him. Some one was over there—at the window, and that some one had softly crossed the room. Bob made an involuntary movement, turning in bed to see plainer, when with a slight sound of suppressed surprise, the some one almost magically disappeared. Bob couldn't tell whether he had gone out of the window, or had sprung back into the room and was now concealing himself behind the heavy curtains. The young man made a sudden rush for the window and grab for the curtain, only to discover there was no one there; nor could he see any one on the balcony, or climbing down. He did see below, however, a skulking figure fast vanishing among the shrubbery. A moment, the thought of the commodore insinuated itself in the young man's bewildered brain, but the commodore would not again be trying to see him (Bob) here, for the very good reason that Dan could not know Bob was here. No one yet knew Bob had returned to Mrs. Ralston's house. The commodore and Clarence no doubt still believed Bob to be shut up in a cute little cubby-hole with bars.

The skulking figure below, then, could be dissociated from the complicated domestic tangle; his proper place was in that other silent drama, dealing with mysterious peculations. Should Bob climb down, follow and attempt to capture him? Bob had on only his pajamas and already the fellow was far away. He would lead any one a fine chase and Bob hadn't any special desire to go romping over hills in his present attire, or want of attire. If any one caught him doing it, what excuse could he make? That he was chasing an accomplice of a thief inside the house who had probably dropped his glittering booty for his pal to take away? But he (Bob) was supposed to be that inside-operator, himself, and he wouldn't be chasing his own pal. Or again, if he were detected in that sprinting performance by those who didn't know he was supposed to be an inside-operator, but who thought him only a plain crazy man, wouldn't the necessity for his reincarceration be but emphasized? Maybe this latter contingent of his enemies would consider a plain, public insane asylum, without flowers in the window, good enough for him. They, undoubtedly, *would* so conclude if they knew the state of Bob's private fortune, which certainly did not justify private institutions.

A slight noise behind him drove all these considerations from Bob's mind. He dove at once in the direction of the sound, only to fall over his grip, and as he sprawled, not heroically, in the dark, his door was opened and closed almost noiselessly. Exasperated, he gathered himself together and made for the door. Throwing it back, he gazed down the hall, only to see a figure swiftly vanishing around a dimly-lighted corner. Bob couldn't make out whether it was a man or a woman, but seeing no one else in the hall, he impetuously and recklessly darted after it. When he reached the corner, however, the figure was gone.

Bob stood in a quandary. There were a good many different doors around that corner. Through which one had his mysterious visitor vanished? If he but knew, he felt certain he could place his hand on the much wanted individual who was making such a nuisance of himself in social circles. He might be able to rid society of one of those essentially modern pests, and at the same time lift the mantle of suspicion from himself. At least, he would be partly rehabilitated. Later, he might complete the process. And oh, to have her once more see him as he was.

He was sorely tempted to try a door. He even put his hand on the knob of the door nearest the corner. The figure must have turned in here; he couldn't have gone farther without Bob's having caught sight of him. At least, Bob felt almost sure of this conclusion, having attained that corner with considerable celerity, himself.

Almost on the point of turning the knob, prudence bade Bob to pause. Suppose he made a mistake? Suppose, for example, he stumbled upon Gee-gee's room, or Gid-up's? The perspiration started on Bob's brow. Gee-gee would be quite capable of hanging on to him and then raising a row, just for publicity purposes. She would make "copy" out of anything, that girl would. Then, if it wasn't Gee-gee's room, it might be Mrs. Van's. Fancy his invading the privacy of that austere lady's boudoir! Bob's hand shook slightly and the knob rattled a trifle; he hastily released it. To his horror a voice called out.

"Any one there?"

It was Gee-gee. Bob stood still, not daring to stir, lest Gee-gee, with senses alert, should hear him and come out and find him. He prayed devoutly not to be "found." It was bad enough to be crazy, and to be a social buccaneer, without having Miss Gerald look upon him as an intrigant, a Don Juan and a Jonathan Wild all rolled into one. Bob wanted to flee the worst way, but still he thought it better to contain himself and stand there like a wooden man a few moments longer.

"Any one there?" repeated Gee-gee.

A neighboring door opened and one of the last men Bob wanted to see, under the circumstances, looked out. It was the hammer-thrower and his honest face expressed a world of wonder, incredulity and reproach, as he beheld and recognized Bob, who didn't know what to do, or to say. He certainly didn't want to say anything though, having no desire to agitate Miss Gee-gee any further. Fortunately, the hammer-thrower seemed too amazed for words. He just kept looking and looking. "Where on earth did you come from?" his glance seemed to say. "Are you the ghost of Bob Bennett? And if you aren't, what are you doing here, before a lady's door, at this time of night?"

Disapproval now became mixed with indecision in the hammer-thrower's glance. He seemed trying to make up his mind whether or not it was a case demanding forcible measures on his part. Was it his duty to spring upon Bob, then and there, and "show him up" before the world? Bob read the thought. In another moment Gee-gee might come to the door, and then—? Bob suddenly and desperately determined to throw himself upon the mercy of the hammer-thrower. Indeed, he had no choice.

Quickly he moved to the door where his hated rival stood and as quickly pushed by him and entered that person's room. At the same moment Gee-gee unlocked her door. Bob couldn't see her, though, as he was now thankfully swallowed up in the depths of a recess in the hammer-thrower's room. Gee-gee peeked out. She met the eye of the hammer-thrower who had modestly withdrawn most of his person back into his apartment and who now suffered only a fraction of his face to be revealed to Gee-gee at that unseemly hour and place, and under such unseemly circumstances.

"I beg your pardon," said the hammer-thrower deferentially, and in a very low tone, "but did you call out?"

"Yes, I thought I heard some one at my door."

Bob hardly breathed. Would the hammer-thrower hale him forth? Would he toss him—or try to—right out into the hall at Gee-gee's feet?

"I—I don't see any one," said the hammer-thrower hesitatingly, and still in a very low tone. His hesitation, however, told Bob he had considered or was still considering that forcible policy.

"I certainly thought I did hear some one," observed Gee-gee, matching the other's tones. His voice seemed to imply that it might be as well not to arouse any others of the household and Gee-gee involuntarily fell in with the suggestion.

"You—" Again, however, that awful hesitation! The hammer-thrower had no reason to like Bob, for did he not know that young gentleman had the presumption to adore Miss Gerald? Still the apparently more successful suitor for Gwendoline's hand had a sportsmanlike instinct. He'd been brought up to be conscientious. He had been educated to be gentlemanly and considerate. Perhaps he was asking himself now if it might not be more sportsmanlike not to denounce Bob, then and there, but to give him, at least, a chance to explain? "You—you must be mistaken," said the hammer-thrower, after a pause, in a low tense whisper.

"You're sure it wasn't you?" murmured Gee-gee softly but suspiciously and eying the other's open and trustworthy countenance.

"I?" For a moment Bob thought now, indeed, had come the time to eject him, but—"Is that a reasonable conjecture?" the other murmured back.

Gee-gee pondered. "No, it ain't," she confessed, at length. Locked double-doors separated her room and the hammer-thrower's. He would surely have used a skeleton key on those doors were he the guilty party, instead of going out into the hall to try to get in that way. "I got to thinking of that swell burglar who is going the rounds, before I went to sleep," murmured Gee-gee, "and I may have been dreaming of him! Sorry to have disturbed you." And Gee-gee closed her door very quietly.

She thought she must have been mistaken about the intruder. Anyhow, there wasn't much excitement for an actress any more, in being robbed. That advertising stunt had been so overworked that even the provincial dramatic critics yawned and tossed the advance man's little yarn of "jewels lost" right into an unsympathetic waste-basket. A scandal in high life was always more efficacious. No one ever got tired of scandals and city editors simply clamored for "more." So Gee-gee composed herself for sleep again. She had reason to be satisfied, for had not she and Gid-up, who roomed with her, sat up late and arranged final details before retiring?

Gid-up would say: "We'll make it like this." And Gee-gee would answer: "No, like this." Of course, Gee-gee's way was better. Upon a slender thread of fact she fashioned, as Dickie had feared, a most wonderful edifice of fancy. She had mapped out a case that would startle even dear old New York. "Better do it good, if we're going to do it at all," she had said. Gid-up had been a little doubtful at first, but she always did what Gee-gee told her to in the end. And Gee-gee knew she could depend upon Gid-up's memory, for once the latter had had a small part. She had to say: "Send for the doctor" and she had never been known to get mixed up and say: "Send for the police," or for the undertaker, or anything equally ridiculous. Having thoroughly rehearsed her lines, she would stick to them like a major. When Mrs. Dan and Mrs. Clarence and the two G's should get together on the morrow, the largest anticipations of the two former ladies would be realized. Gee-gee wouldn't have Mrs. Dan disappointed for the world. Gid-up was rather afraid of Mrs. Clarence; however, she had been batted about by so many rough stage-managers and cranky musical-directors, she could stand almost anything.

But what about Bob?

That young gentleman, now seated in the hammer-thrower's room, had frankly revealed what had happened to bring him out in the hall. In a low tone he told why he had approached Gee-gee's door and what had been in his mind when he had placed his hand on the knob. The hammer-thrower, if not appearing particularly impressed by Bob's story, listened gravely; occasionally he shook his head. It wasn't, on the whole, a very reasonable-sounding yarn. Truth certainly sounded stranger than fiction in this instance. Bob couldn't very well blame the other for not believing. Still he (Bob) owed him that explanation. Though he (Bob) might detest him as the man who would probably rob him of Miss Gerald's hand, still the fact remained that the hammer-thrower appeared at present in the guise of his (Bob's) savior. Bob couldn't get away from this unpleasant conclusion. He didn't want to have anything to do with the other and yet here he was in his room, actually being shielded by him. The situation was, indeed, well-nigh intolerable.

The hammer-thrower studied Bob with quiet earnest eyes, and the latter had to acknowledge to himself that the man's face was strong and capable. If Miss Gerald married him—as seemed not unlikely— she would, at any rate, not get a weak man. He was about as big as Bob, though not so reckless-looking. Bob was handsomer, in his dashing way, but some girls, sensibly inclined, would prefer what might appear a more reliable type. The hammer-thrower looked so sure of himself and his ground he inspired confidence. He looked too sure of his ground now, as regards Bob.

"It won't do," he said with his usual directness to Bob, when the latter had finished explaining. "Sounds a little fishy! I'm sorry, old chap, but I shall have to have time to think it all over. And then I'll try to decide what is best to be done. You say you were unjustly incarcerated in a private sanatorium." Bob hadn't explained the circumstances—who had "incarcerated" him and why. "That you were incarcerated at all is a matter of regret."

"To you?" said Bob cynically.

"Of course." Firmly, but with faint surprise. "You didn't think I rejoiced at your misfortune, did you?"

"I didn't know. I thought it possible."

The hammer-thrower's heavy brows drew together. "You seem to have a little misconception of my character," he observed with a trace of formality. "You were incarcerated, apparently, *pro bono publico*. I had no hand in it. If I had been consulted, I should have hesitated some time before expressing an opinion."

"Thanks," said Bob curtly. Such generous reserve was rather galling, coming from this quarter.

"I'm afraid you don't mean that," replied the other. "And it's a bad habit to say what you don't mean. However, we are drifting from the subject. You will pardon me for not swallowing, *a capite ad calcem*, that little Münchhausen explanation of yours."

"I don't care whether you swallow it head, neck and breeches, or not," returned Bob. The other had taken a classical course at college, and Bob conceived he was ponderously trying to show off, just to be annoying. He was adopting a doubly irritating and classical manner of calling Bob a liar. And that young man was not accustomed to being called that—at least, of yore! Maybe he would have to stand it now. It seemed so. "You're like a good many other people I've met lately," said Bob, not without a touch of weariness as well as bitterness. "You don't know the truth when you hear it."

The hammer-thrower drew up his heavy shoulders. "No use abusing me, old chap," he said in even well-poised tones. "Am I at fault for your unpopularity? Indeed"—as if arguing with himself in his slow heavy fashion—"I fail to understand why you have made yourself unpopular. You seem to have proceeded with deliberate intention. However, that is irrelevant. You say there was some one in your room, or rather the room you were supposed to have vacated; but to which you have unaccountably returned—not, I imagine, by way of the front door." Severely. "And after entering in burglarious fashion you pursued a phantom. The phantom vanished, leaving you in a compromising position. You expect people to believe that?" Shaking his head.

"I should be surprised if they did," answered Bob gloomily. "I suppose you'll tell everybody to-morrow."

"That's the question," said the other seriously. "What is my duty in the matter? I don't want to do you an irreparable injury, yet appearances certainly seem to indicate that you—" He hesitated.

"Never mind the Latin for it," said Bob. "Plain Anglo-Saxon will do. Call me a thief."

"It's an ugly word," said the other reluctantly, "and—well, I don't wish to be hasty. My father always told me to help a man whenever I could; not to shove him down. And maybe—" He paused. There was really a nice expression on his strong face.

"Oh, you think I may be only a young offender—a juvenile in crime?" exclaimed Bob bitterly.

"The words are your own," observed the other. "To tell you the truth," seriously, "I hardly know what to think. It is all too extraordinary—too unexpected. I'll have to ponder on it. The profs, at college always said I had the champion slow brain. The peculiar part to me is," that puzzled look returning to his heavy features, "I can't understand why you're making people think what they do of you? Frankly, I don't believe you're 'dippy.' You were always rather—just what is the word?—'mercurial'—yes; that will do. But your head looks right enough to me."

"What's the Latin for 'Thank you'?" said Bob.

"Do you really think this is a trivial matter?" asked the other, bending a stronger glance upon his visitor. "I believe you are somewhat obligated to me. Please bear that in mind." With quiet dignity. "As I was saying, your conduct since coming here, seems to baffle explanation—that is, the right one. I wonder what is your

'lay,' anyhow? What's the idea? I like to be able to grasp people."
Forcefully. "And you escape me. I can't get at the tangible in you.
Nor"—with a sudden quick glance—"can Miss Gerald—"

"Suppose we leave her name out," said Bob sharply. "You've done
me a favor which I ought not to have accepted. And I tell you frankly
I'd rather have accepted it from any one else in the world."

"I think I understand," replied the other quietly, with no show of
resentment on his heavy features. "Have a cigar?" Indicating a box
on the table.

"I'd rather not."

"Very well!"

For some moments Bob sat in moody silence. Then suddenly he got
up.

"Am I to be permitted to return to my room?" he asked.

"I believe I told you I would consider your case," said the hammer-
thrower.

And Bob passed out. He regained his room without mishap, which
rather surprised him. He almost expected to be intercepted by the
monocle-man but nothing of the kind happened.

CHAPTER XVI—PLAYING WITH BOB

It took a great deal of courage for Bob to go down to breakfast the next morning. In fact, he had never done anything before in his life that demanded so much courage. He pictured his entrance, anticipating what would happen; he didn't try to deceive himself. The monocle-man would tap him on the shoulder. "You are my prisoner," he would say. And then it would be "exit" for Bob amid the exclamations and in the face of the accumulated staring of the company.

Bob wasn't going to play the craven now, though, so he marched down-stairs and into the breakfast-room, his head well up. With that smile on his lips and the frosty light in his blue eyes, he looked not unlike a young Viking fearlessly presenting a bold brow to the enemy while his ship is sinking beneath him. He acted just as if he hadn't been away and as if nothing had happened.

"Good-morning, people," he said in his cheeriest.

For a moment there was a tombstone silence while Bob, not seeming to notice it, dropped down in a convenient place at the table. His vis-a-vis, as luck, or ill-luck would have it, was the monocle-man. Bob felt the shivers stealing over him. But the monocle-man, too, acted as if nothing had happened. He didn't get up and tap Bob on the shoulder. Perhaps he wished to finish his breakfast first.

"Aw!—Have some toast," he observed to Bob. "Mrs. Ralston's toast is really delicious."

"No," said Bob airily. "I don't like that English kind of toast. Makes me think of rusk! No taste to it! Give me good old American toast with plenty of butter on it."

"Aw!" said the monocle-man.

Bob didn't stop there. He appealed to the bishop and carried the discussion on to the doctor. He even went so far, a daredevil look in his sanguine blue eyes now, as to ask Miss Gerald's opinion. Miss

Gerald, however, pretended not to hear. Her devoted admirer was close at hand and Bob saw the hammer-thrower's brows knit at sight of him. Bob in his new mood didn't care a straw now and looked straight back at the hammer-thrower, as if daring him to do his worst. For an instant he thought the hammer-thrower was going to say something, but he didn't. Perhaps second thought told him it would be better taste to wait, for he lifted his heavy shoulders with rather a contemptuous or pitying shrug and paid no further attention to luckless Bob.

The latter kept up a gay conversation between bites, professing to be quite unaware of a certain extraordinary reticence with which his light persiflage was received. He looked around to see if Gee-gee and Gid-up were anywhere visible and saw that they were not. This did not surprise him, as theatrical ladies are usually late risers and like to breakfast in their rooms; nor would they be apt to mingle promiscuously with the other guests. Mrs. Ralston, Mrs. Dan and Mrs. Clarence were also not about. Bob was thankful Mrs. Ralston needed most of the morning by herself, or with sundry experts, to beautify; he didn't care to see his hostess just yet. It was hard enough to meet her fair niece, Miss Gerald, under the circumstances.

"I understand we have two new arrivals in the professional entertaining line," said Bob to the monocle-man.

"Aw!—how interesting!" replied the other. Bob couldn't get much of a "rise" out of him, though unvaryingly affable in his manner toward the young man. "Try some of this marmalade—do—it's Scotch, you know. All marmalade ought to be Scotch. Dislike intensely the English make!"

"How unpatriotic!" said Bob cynically. Really, the monocle-man did it very well. He was a fine imitation.

"Aw!" he said once more.

And then Bob began to play with him. Dear old dad who was somewhat of a bibliomaniac had, on one or two of Bob's vacation trips to London, introduced the lad to many quaint, out-of-the-way nooks and corners. Now Bob drew on the source of information thus gleaned and angled with his one-eye-glassed neighbor. But the monocle-man fenced beautifully; he knew more than Bob. And when the latter had exhausted himself, the monocle-man, with a few twinkles behind his staring window-pane, played with Bob. He showed him as a mere child for ignorance of the subject, and drawled so brilliantly that some of the others became interested, though professing not to see that Bob was there. When the monocle-man had finished, Bob felt abashed. He gazed upon the other with new and wondrous respect. He had attempted the infantile and amateurish game of unmasking the other—of exhibiting his crass ignorance and letting the others draw their own conclusions—and he had been literally overwhelmed in his efforts.

Having shown Bob the futility of trying to play with him, the monocle-man again offered Bob the marmalade. His manner of doing it made Bob think of a jailer who believed in the humane treatment of prisoners and who liked to see them well-fed. Bob for the second time refused the marmalade and did it most emphatically. Whereupon the monocle-man smiled.

At that moment Bob met the gaze of the temperamental young thing. There were dark rings under her eyes and she looked paler than he had ever seen her. Also, there was a certain fascinated wonder, not unmixed with some deeper feeling, in her expression. She was, no doubt, absolutely astounded to see Bob there, and talking with the monocle-man. Bob surmised she would be waiting for him somewhere later to express herself, and he was not mistaken. Bob got up. As he did so, he glanced at the monocle-man. Would he be permitted to go, or would the denouement now happen? Would the other, alas, arise?

He did nothing of the kind. He let Bob have a little more line. He even suffered him to walk away, at the same time smiling once more at vacancy or the rack of toast. Of course the temperamental young thing hailed Bob shortly after he was out of the room. He expected that. She came hurrying up to him, excitement and terror in her eyes.

"Flee!" she whispered.

"I won't do it," answered Bob sturdily.

"Why did you come back?" Agitatedly, "What a rash thing to do! Like walking into the lions' den."

"Well, the principal lion was nice and polite, anyhow."

"Could you not see he was only just"—she sought for a word—"dallying with you?"

"He made me see that," Bob confessed rather gloomily. "He made me feel like thirty cents. I guess he's got my goat. And to think I thought him a blamed fool. I tell you I'm learning something these days; I'm taking a course they don't have in college, all right."

"Why do you waste time talking?" said the girl. "Every moment is precious. Go, or you are lost."

"That sounds like the stage," replied Bob.

She came closer, her temperamental gaze burning. "Will this make you serious?" she asked almost fiercely. "I told."

"Eh?"

"I told all," she repeated.

"You did?"

"Yes."

"When?"

"Last night."

"Hum!" said Bob. "That makes it a little worse, that is all."

"I was mad," she said, "at the way you—you—"

"I think I understand."

"Why—why don't you get angry and—"

"And curse you the way they do in plays?" He laughed a little mirthlessly. "What's the use? It wouldn't do any good if I dragged you around by the hair."

"It's just that attitude of yours," she said, breathing hard, "that has made me perfectly furious."

"Who'd you tell?" Bob eyed her contemplatively.

"Lord Stan—The monocle-man, as you call him."

"Whew!" Bob whistled. "You went straight to headquarters, didn't you?"

"He came up to me on the porch just after you had left, and—and—"

"It's quite plain," said Bob gently. "You couldn't hold in. Don't know as I ought to blame you much."

"I wish you wouldn't act like that," she returned passionately. "Don't you hate me?"

He looked at her from his superior height. "No. Now that I think of it, you only did the right and moral thing. After all"—he seemed to be speaking from the hammer-thrower's high judicial plane—"it was your duty to tell."

"Duty!" she shot back at him. "I didn't do it for that, or"—with sudden scorn—"because it was the moral thing. I did it because—because you—you had hurt me and—and I wanted to hurt you the worst way—the very worst way I could—"

"Well, that sounds very human," replied Bob soothingly. "It's the old law. Eye for an eye! Tit for tat! *Quid pro quo!*" That hammer-thrower was getting him into the Latin habit.

"You must not speak like that. You *must* hate me—despise me—I betrayed you—betrayed—"

Bob looked at her sympathetically. She really was suffering. "Oh, no, you didn't. You only thought you did," he said.

"I did! I did! And afterward I felt like Salome with the head of John the Baptist."

Bob twisted his handsome head and lifted a hand to his neck. "Well, it's really not so bad as that," he returned in a tone intended to be consoling. "Anyhow, it's very brave of you to come and tell me about it."

"Brave!" she scoffed, the temperamental breast rising. "Why, I just blurted it all right out—how I discovered you in my room—how I turned on the light and how you dropped the brooch to the floor!"

For a few moments both were silent. Then Bob spoke: "How'd it be, if we called bygones, bygones, and just be friends?" he said gravely. "Honestly, I believe I could like you an awful lot as a friend."

"Don't!" she said hoarsely. "Or—or I can't hold in. My! but you are good."

"Isn't that the sound of music?" said Bob suddenly.

"I—I believe it is."

"A tango, by jove! Think of tangoing right after breakfast! Some one *is* beginning early. What are we coming to in these degenerate days?" Bob wanted to take her thoughts off that other disagreeable subject. His own sudden and unexpected appearance had, no doubt, been quite upsetting to those other guests. That tango music had a wild irresponsible sound, as if the some one who was banging the concert-grand in the big music salon was endeavoring to turn the general trend of fancy into more symphonious channels. He, or she, was a musical good Samaritan. Bob held out a ceremonious arm to the temperamental young thing. "Shall we?" he said. "Why not?"

"You mean—?"

"Tango with me? That is, if you are not above tangoing with a—"

She slipped an uncertain little hand on his arm.

"It may be my last, for a long time," he said gaily. "While we live, let us live."

But when they entered they saw it was the man with the monocle who sat at the big, wonderfully carved piano. His fingers were fairly flying; his face was a bit more twisted up to keep the monocle from falling off, while he was flinging his hands about over the keys. At sight of him, the temperamental little thing breathed quickly and would have drawn back, but Bob drew her forward. The monocle-man's face did not change as he glanced over his shoulder to regard them; he had a faculty for hitting the right keys without looking. Bob put a big reassuring arm about a slim waist. He tangoed only to show the temperamental little thing that he forgave her. But her feet were not so light as ordinarily and the dance rather dragged. Once Bob looked down; why, she wasn't much bigger than a child.

"Friends?" he asked.

Her little hand clutched tighter for answer, and the monocle-man played more madly. It was as if he were making the puppets fly around while he pulled the strings. He seemed having the best kind of a time. There was now a whimsical look in his eyes as they followed Bob.

That was one of the longest days Bob ever knew. The temperamental thing had told him they were coming to arrest him. Well, why didn't they? His appearing unexpectedly on the spot like that may have caused them to change their minds. He included in the "them" Mrs. Ralston and her niece and he could only conclude they all meant to "dally" with him, in Miss Dolly's phraseology, a little longer. But surely they had enough evidence to go right ahead and let justice (?) take its course. What the temperamental little thing had confessed would be quite sufficient in itself, for their purpose.

Bob began to get impatient; he didn't like being "dallied" with. In his desperate mood, he desired to meet the issue at once and since "it" was bound to happen, he wanted it to happen right off. Then he would robustly proclaim his innocence—aye, and fight for it with all his might. He was in a fighting mood.

Mrs. Ralston's demeanor toward him—when in the natural order of events he was obliged to meet that lady—added to his feeling of utter helplessness. She, like the monocle-man, acted as if nothing had happened, seeming to see nothing extraordinary or surprising in his being there. She treated him just as if he hadn't been away and talked in the most natural manner about the weather or other commonplace topics. She was graciousness itself, even demanding playfully if he hadn't thought of any more French compliments?

Bob stammered he had not. The fact that Miss Gerald was near and overheard all they said didn't add to his mental composure. Gwendoline's violet eyes had such a peculiar look. Bob hoped and prayed she would preserve that manner of cold and haughty aloofness. He wouldn't have exchanged a word with her now for all the world, if he had had any choice in the matter. Did she divine his inward shrinking from any further talk with her? Did she realize she was the one especial person Bob didn't want to converse with, under the circumstances? It may be she did so realize; also, that she deliberately sought to add to his discomfiture. Possibly, she felt no punishment could be too great for one who had sunk so low as he had.

At any rate, the day was yet young when, like a proud princess, she stood suddenly before him. Bob had taken refuge in that summer-house where she had proposed (ha! ha!) to him. He had been noting that Mrs. Ralston seemed to have several new gardeners working for her and it had flashed across his mind that these gardeners were of the monocle-man type. They were imitation gardeners. One kept a furtive eye on Bob. He was under surveillance. Now he could understand why the monocle-man let him flutter this way and that, with seeming unconcern. Oh, he was being dallied with, sure enough! That monocle-man was argus-eyed. Bob had had a sample of his cleverness at the breakfast-table.

Miss Gerald's shadow fell abruptly at Bob's feet. He saw it before he saw her—a radiant, accusing patrician presence. The girl carried a golf stick, but there was no caddy in sight.

"Mr. Bennett," said Miss Gerald, with customary directness, "do you know who poisoned my aunt's dog?"

Bob scrambled to his feet awkwardly. Her loveliness alone was enough to embarrass him. "No," he said.

"He was poisoned that night you left," she said, and went on studying him.

Bob pondered heavily. If the dog had been killed with a golf stick for example, he might have been to blame. "You are sure he was poisoned?" he asked with an effort.

"Certainly." In surprise.

"Well, I didn't do it," said Bob.

"Were you in any way responsible for it?" She stood like an angel of the flaming sword in the doorway, where the sunlight framed her figure. She rather intoxicated poor Bob.

"Not to my knowledge," he said. Of course the commodore might have poisoned the dog, but it was unlikely. Probably that inside-operator, or his outside pal had "done the deed." A dog would be in their way.

Miss Gerald considered. "There is another question I should like to ask you, Mr. Bennett," she said presently.

"Go on," returned Bob, with dark forebodings.

"Are you a sleep-walker?"

"No."

"Then why do you go wandering around nights when every one else has retired? Last night, for example?"

"So that hammer-thrower told you, did he?" remarked Bob. "I thought he would."

"Do you blame him?"

"Oh, I suppose it was his duty." Every one seemed "telling" on Bob just at present.

"You do not deny it?"

"Why should I?"

"Then we may accept his version of the story?"

"Yes. I presume it was correct."

Again Miss Gerald remained thoughtful and Bob glanced out toward the gardeners. One of them seemed to have edged nearer. Bob smiled a little glumly. After having caught him in the web, the spiders were now winding the strands around and around him. Spiders do that when they don't want to devour their victim right off. They mummify the victim, as it were, and tuck him away for the morrow.

"Why"—the accusing presence was again speaking—"did you go down-stairs that first night of your arrival, after all the household had retired?"

Bob would have given a great deal not to answer that, but he had to. "I was showing some people out."

"Your accomplices?"

"They might be called that." Miserably. He wouldn't "give away" Dan and the others, unless he had to—unless truth compelled him to designate them by name as his accomplices.

"Are you aware, Mr. Bennett, of the seriousness of your answer?"

"Yes, I know. But how did you know—that I went down-stairs?"

"I thought I heard some one go down. And then I got up and you went by my door, and I looked out, ever so quietly. You went in Dolly's room and she woke up and caught you trying to take her brooch."

Bob was silent. What was the use of talking?

"Well, why don't you speak?"

"It is true I went in Miss Dolly's room, but I thought it was my room," said Bob monotonously. "It was a mistake." And Bob told how the brooch happened to fall to the floor. Strange to say, truth didn't ring in his accents. He hadn't much confidence at that moment in the old saw that truth is mighty and will prevail. Truth wasn't mighty; it was a monster that sucked your heart's blood. And Bob gazed once more with that famished look upon Miss Gerald. He found her a joy to the eye. Though she stood in a practical pose, the curves of her gracious and proud young figure were like ardent lines of poetry in a matutinal and passionate hymn to beauty. And Bob's lips straightway yearned to sing hexameters to loveliness in the abstract—and in the flesh—instead of plodding along half-heartedly through unconvincing and purposeless explanations.

"You certainly do look fine to-day!" burst from Bob. It wasn't exactly a hexameter nor yet an iambic mode of expression. But it had to come out.

Roses blossomed on the girl's proud cheek. Bob's explosive and uncontrollable ardency would have been disconcerting, under any circumstances, but under such as those of the present—Miss Gerald's eyes flashed.

"Isn't—isn't that rather irrelevant?" she said after a moment's pause.

"I—yes, I guess it is," confessed Bob, and his head slowly fell. He looked at the hard marble pavement.

A moment the girl stood with breast stirring, like an indignant goddess. "Have you—have you any information to volunteer?" she said at length icily.

"Oh, I don't have to volunteer," answered Bob. And then rushed on to a Niagara of disaster. "Why don't you ask that hammer-thrower? I suppose you'd believe *anything*"—he couldn't keep back the bitter jealousy—"he tells you."

An instant eyes met eyes. Bob's now were stubborn, if forlorn and miserable. They braved the indignant, outraged violet ones. He even laughed, savagely, moodily. What would he not have given if she would only believe him, instead of—? But it was not to be. Yet this girl had his very soul. His miserable and forlorn eyes told her that.

Whose eyes would have turned first, in that visual contest is a matter of uncertainty, for just then the enthusiastic voice of Gee-gee was heard "through the land."

"Why, Mr. Bennett—you here? So glad to see you!"

Bob forgot all about heroics. Gee-gee drifted in as if she were greeting an old and very dear friend, instead of a casual acquaintance, upon whom, indeed, she had rather forced herself, on a certain memorable evening. Bob wilted. When he recovered a little, Miss Gerald was gone. Below them the gardener who had caught Bob's eye now drew a bit nearer. Bob turned on Gee-gee.

CHAPTER XVII—A GOOD DEAL OF GEE-GEE

"See here," he said rather savagely, "this has got to stop."

Gee-gee stared. "Bless its little heart, what is it talking about?"

"You know," said Bob. The fact that he now saw Gwendoline Gerald rejoined afar by the hammer-thrower did not improve his temper.

"Pardon me," returned Gee-gee, tossing her auburn hair, "if I fail to connect. Mrs. Ralston has been good enough to treat us as her regular guests. And, indeed, why shouldn't she?" With much dignity. "But if you feel I ain't good enough to speak to your Lord Highmightiness, except at stage doors and alleys and roof gardens—" Cuttingly.

"This isn't a question of social amenities," said Bob. Gee-gee didn't know what "amenities" meant and that made *her* madder. "You've come down here to raise a regular hornet's nest."

Gee-gee sat down. She was so mad she had to do something. She wanted to slap Bob's face, but she couldn't do that. As Mrs. Ralston's guest she couldn't give way to her natural and primitive impulses. Her gown, modishly tight all over, strained almost to bursting point; it seemed to express the state of her feelings. A high-heeled shoe, encasing a pink-stockinged foot, agitated itself like a flag in a gale.

"I like that," she gasped. "And who are you to talk to me like that? Maybe you think this is a rehearsal."

"For argument's sake, I'll own I'm not much account just at present," said Bob. "Be that as it may, I'm going to try to stop the mischief you are up to, if I can." He didn't know how he would stop it; he was talking more to draw Gee-gee out than for any other purpose. Bob's own testimony, as to certain occurrences on that memorable roof-garden evening, wouldn't amount to much. The lawyers could impeach it even if they let him (Bob) testify at all in those awful divorce cases that were pending. But they probably wouldn't let him take the witness-stand if he was a prisoner. Bob didn't know quite what was the law governing the admissibility of testimony in a case like his.

Gee-gee shifted her mental attitude. She was getting her second breath and caution whispered to her to control herself. This handsome young gentleman had been the most indifferent member of the quartet on that inauspicious occasion on the roof; indeed, he had yawned in the midst of festivities. Bob, in love, cared not for show-girls or ponies. He had even tried to discourage Dan and the others in their zest for innocent enjoyment. Gee-gee now eyed Bob more critically. As a young-man-sure-of-himself, he had impressed her on that other occasion! Instinct had told her to avoid Bob and select Dan. Now that same instinct told her it might be better to temporize with this blunt-speaking young gentleman—to "sound" him.

"You sure have got me floating," observed Gee-gee in more lady-like accents. "I'm way up in the air. Throw out a few sand-bags and let's hit the earth."

"That's easy," said Bob. "Do you deny you're down here to raise Ned?"

"Do I deny it?" remarked Gee-gee with flashing eyes. "Do I? We are down here to fill a little professional engagement. We are down here on account of our histrionic talents." A sound came from Bob's throat. Gee-gee professed not to notice it. "We are paid a fee—not a small one—to come down here, to do privately our little turn which was the hit of the piece and the talk of Broadway."

"Bosh!" said Bob coolly. Gee-gee looked dangerous. Once more the pink-stockinged ankle began to swing agitatedly, and again reckless Bob narrowly escaped a slap in the face. "Mrs. Dan and Mrs. Clarence got Mrs. Ralston to ask you down here," he went on. "You weren't asked on account of your histrionic ability. You were asked because it was the only feasible way to get you beyond other strong, I may even say desperate, and to them, inimical influences. Mrs.

Ralston isn't the only one who is financing your little rural expedition. I guess you know what I mean?"

"Nix!" said Gee-gee. "You've got me up in the air again. Turn the little wheel around and let the car come down. This ain't Sunday, and if I was taking a little Coney-Island treat, I wouldn't choose you for my escort."

"It certainly isn't Sunday in the sense of a day of rest," remarked Bob gloomily. By this time the hammer-man and Miss Gerald were beyond his range of vision. But he would not think of them; he must not. He had a duty to perform here; maybe it would do no good, but it was his duty to try. "That publicity racket is all right up to a certain point," he said, bending his reproachful eyes upon Gee-gee. "But when it comes to smashing reputations, stretching the truth, and injuring others irreparably—all for a little cheap nauseating notoriety—Well"—Bob hit straight from the shoulder—"I tell you it's rotten. And I, for one, shall do what I can to show up the whole conspiracy. That's what it is. It would be different if you were going to tell what was so, but you aren't. It isn't in the cards."

"I don't know what you're talking about." Gee-gee's tight dress nearly exploded now. The blood had receded from her face and left it a mottled cream while her greenish eyes glowed like opals. Her expression was animalistic. It seemed to say she would like to crush something beneath those high heels and grind them into it.

"Yes, you do," said Bob. "And it will be a frame-up for poor old Dan and Clarence, too!" Dickie's description of what was going to happen recurred to him poignantly. "I tell you it's a wicked cruel thing to do. I repeat, it's rotten."

If he thought he could overwhelm Gee-gee by a display of superior masculine strength and moral force, he was mistaken. Gee-gee wasn't that kind of a girl. She had some force herself, though whether of the moral kind is another matter.

"'Wicked!' 'Rotten!' 'Cheap!'" she repeated slowly, but breathing hard. "Listen to the infant! 'Rotten!'" She lingered on the word as if it had a familiar sound. "Well, what is life, anyhow?" she flung out suddenly at the six-foot "infant." "Maybe you think this theater business is like going to Sunday-school—that all we have to do is to hold goody-goody hands and sing those salvation songs! Salvation! Gee!" And Gee-gee folded her arms. She seemed to meditate. "You know what kind of salvation a girl gets down on old Broadway?" she scoffed. "Aren't the men nice and kind? Don't they take you by the hand and say: 'Come on, little girl, I'll give you a helping hand.' Oh, yes, they give you a helping hand. But it isn't 'up.' It's all 'down.' And every one wants to see how deep they can make it. Say, Infant, I was born in one of those avenues with letters. People like these"—looking toward the house—"don't know nothing about that kind of an avenue. It ought to be called a rotten alley. That's where I learned what 'rotten' meant. Nice young gentlemen like you who toddled about with nursie in the park can't tell *me*."

Bob tried not to look small; he endeavored to maintain his dignity. He was almost sorry he had got Gee-gee started. The conversation was leading into unexpected channels. "Why, I toddled about in rottenness," went on Gee-gee. "Gutters were my playground." Dreamily. She seemed to be forgetting her resentment in these childhood recollections. "Sometimes I slept in cellar doorways, with the rotten cabbages all around. But they and all the rest of the spoiled things seemed to agree with me. I've thrived on rottenness, Infant!" Bob winced. "It's all that some girls get. Men!" And Gee-gee laughed. Here was a topic she could dilate on. Again the opal eyes gleamed tigerishly. "I've got a lot of cause to love 'em. Oh, ain't they particular about *their* reputations!" Gee-gee's chuckle was fiendish. "Poor, precious little dears! Be careful and don't get a teeny speck of smudge on their snowy white wings! My! look out! don't splash 'em! Or, if you do, rub it off quick so the people in church won't see it. But when it comes to us"—Gee-gee showed her teeth. "I learned when I was in the gutter that I had to fight. Sometimes I had to fight with dogs for a crust. Sometimes with boys who were worse still. Later, with men who were worst of all. And," said Gee-gee, again tossing her auburn mane, "I'm still fighting, Infant!"

"Which means," said Bob slowly, overlooking these repeated insults to his dignity, "you aren't here just to exhibit those histrionic talents you talked about?"

Gee-gee laughed. She was feeling better-natured now that she had relieved herself by speaking of some of those "wrongs" she and her sex had undoubtedly to endure. There were times when Gee-gee just had to moralize; it was born in her to do so. And she liked particularly to grill the men, and after the grilling—usually to the receptive and sympathetic Gid-up—she particularly liked, also, to go out and angle for one. And after he had taken the hook—the deeper the better—Gee-gee dearly loved the piscatorial sport that came later, of watching the rushes, the wild turnings, the frenzied leaps.

She even began to eye the infant now with sleepy green eyes. But no hook for him! He wasn't hungry. He wouldn't even smell of a bait. Gee-gee felt this, having quite an instinct in such matters. Perhaps experience, too, had helped make her a good fisherwoman. So she didn't even bother making any casts for Bob. But she answered him sweetly enough, having now recovered her poise and being more sure of her ground:

"It doesn't mean anything of the sort. Our act has been praised in a number of the newspapers, I would have you understand."

"All right," said Bob, as strenuously as he was capable of speaking. "I only wanted you to know that between you and me it will be— fight!"

This was sheer bluff, but he thought it might deter Gee-gee a little. It might curb just a bit that lurid imagination of hers.

Gee-gee got up now, laughing musically. Also, she showed once more her white teeth. Then she stretched somewhat robust arms.

"Fight with you?" she scoffed. "Why, you can't fight, Infant! You haven't grown up yet."

Bob had the grace to blush and Gee-gee, about to depart, noticed it. He looked fresh and big and nice to her at that moment, so nice, indeed, that suddenly she did throw out a bait—one of her most brilliant smiles, supplemented by a speaking, sleepy glance. But Bob didn't see the bait. He was like a fish in a pool too deep for her line. Gee-gee shrugged; then she walked away. Snip! That imitation gardener was now among the vines, right underneath where Bob was sitting.

Gee-gee's little act was better than Bob expected it would be. She sang a French song with no more vulgarity than would mask as piquancy and the men applauded loudly. Gee-gee was a success. Gid-up put hers "over," too; then together they did a few new dances not ungracefully. Mrs. Dan's face was rather a study. She was an extremist on the sex question and would take the woman's side against the man every time. Theoretically, she would invite injured innocence right into camp. She reversed that old humbug saying, "The woman did tempt me;" according to her philosophy, man, being naturally not so good as a woman, was entitled to shoulder the bulk of the blame. But when she looked at Gee-gee she may have had her doubts.

She may even have regretted being instrumental in bringing her here at all. And it is not unlikely that Mrs. Clarence may have entertained a few secret regrets also, and doubts as to the application of a broad-minded big way of looking at certain things pertaining to her own sex, when she beheld her of the saucy turned-up nose and brazen freckle. Certain it is, both Mrs. Dan and Mrs. Clarence looked more serious and thoughtful than jubilant. They didn't applaud; they just seemed to, bringing their hands together without making a noise. But both ladies were now committed to the inevitable. Gee-gee and Gid-up, displaying their "histrionic talents," were but calculated to make Mrs. Dan and Mrs. Clarence the more determined to pursue the matter to the bitter end. Among the guests now was a certain legal light. His presence there at this particular time—when the two G's adorned the festivities—might be a mere coincidence; on the other hand it might signify much. He had certainly spent a long time that afternoon talking to Gee-gee and Gid-up. Mrs. Dan and Mrs. Clarence came in contact with them only by proxy.

Bob was a deeply pained spectator of the wordless drama that was being enacted. He, alone, besides those directly involved, knew the tragedy lurking behind the mocking face of comedy. That gay music sounded to Bob like a fugue. He could well believe what it was costing Mrs. Dan and Mrs. Clarence to attain their purpose. They weren't enjoying themselves. It was altogether a miserable business, and almost made Bob forget his own tragedy. A little incident, however, brought the latter once more vividly to mind.

It occurred while Gee-gee, in answer to applause at the conclusion of her dance with Gid-up, was singing another of those risqué, French cafe chantant songs. Bob sat next to the temperamental little thing who was behaving with exemplary consistency. She had been comporting herself in strictly comrade-fashion ever since their last talk, not once overdoing the little chum act. She hadn't asked him for a single kiss or to put his arm about her waist in dark corners. Perhaps she was too anxious on his account for sentimental considerations. She couldn't understand the way things were going—that is, things pertaining to Bob.

"Why *don't* they?" once she whispered to Bob.

He knew what she meant—arrest him? He shook his head. "Dallying," he answered.

"I could just scratch his eyes out," she murmured with excess of loyalty.

"Whose?"

"That monocle-man. You know what I did this afternoon?"

"No." Bob, however, surmised it would be something interesting.

"I went up to that monocle-man and told him every word I had said to him the night before wasn't so."

"You did?" Staring at her.

"Yes, I did." Setting her cherry lips firmly. "I told him I was just trying to fool him and that I would never—never—never testify to such rubbish, if called on to do so."

"But you'll have to," said Bob. "You've got to tell the truth."

"I'd tell whoppers by the bushel to help you," she confided to him unblushingly. "That's the kind of a friend I am."

"But I wouldn't have you. I wouldn't let you," he murmured in mild consternation. "Great Scott! they'd have you up for perjury."

"Oh, no, they wouldn't. I'd do it so cleverly."

"But the monocle-man would testify, too."

"Who do you think a jury would rather believe, me or him?" she demanded confidently. "Especially if I was all dressed up and looked at them, all the time I was testifying."

"Well," said Bob, "I don't believe you could do it, anyhow. Besides, it would be stretching friendship too far. Though you're a jolly little pal to offer to!" She hunched a dainty little shoulder against his strong arm.

"I'd go through fire and water for you," breathed the jolly little pal.

"It's fine of you to say it," answered Bob fervently. "I haven't many friends now, you know. But—but it's impossible, what you propose. It would only get you into trouble. I'd be a big brute to allow that. It would make me out a fine pal, wouldn't it? Besides, it wouldn't do any good. Some one else heard me go into your room and knows all about it. Some one else would fortify what the monocle-man would tell. And her testimony and his would overwhelm yours. And I'd never forgive myself for your being made a victim of your own loyalty."

"Was that some one else Miss Gerald?" asked the jolly little pal quickly.

"Yes," said Bob. As he spoke he glanced toward Miss Gerald.

Gee-gee had now started to sing and nearly every one's head was turned toward the vivacious vocalist. Bob saw Miss Gerald's proud profile. He saw, too, the hammer-thrower, next to her, as usual. On the other side of the hammer-thrower—the side nearer where Gee-gee stood—was the lady who had given Bob the "cold shoulder" a few nights ago at dinner. The hammer-thrower's eyes were naturally turned toward that cold shoulder now, and, as naturally, his gaze should have been bent over it, toward the vocal center of attraction for the moment.

But his gaze had stopped at the shoulder, or something on it. Bob noted that look. For a fraction of a minute, or second, it revealed a sudden new odd intensity as it rested on a lovely string of pearls ornamenting the cold shoulder. And at the same instant a wave of light seemed to sweep over Bob. For that fraction of a minute he seemed strangely, amazingly, to have been afforded a swift glimpse into a soul.

The whole thing was psychic. Bob couldn't have told just how he came to know. But he knew. He was sure now who had taken Mrs. Vanderpool's brooch. Strangely, too, the hammer-thrower, after that fraction of a second's relaxation of vigilance over his inner secret self, should have turned and looked straight toward Bob. His look was now heavy, normal. Bob's was burning.

"You!" his eyes said as plainly as if he had called out the word.

The hammer-thrower's face did not change in the least; nor did his look. He turned his eyes toward the singer with heavy nonchalance and never had his face appeared more honest and trustworthy.

"Oh, you beauty!" murmured Bob admiringly.

"Do you really think she is?" asked the jolly little pal. She thought Bob meant Gee-gee. "Is that the style you like?"

"Thinking of something else," said Bob.

"Some one, you mean?" with slight reproach.

"Pals aren't jealous," he reminded her. "Besides, it was a man."

"Oh!" she said wonderingly.

"For life is but a game of hide-and-seek,"

sang Gee-gee, in the rather execrable French some one had drilled into her.

"Come and catch me," was the refrain.

Bob shook his head. He didn't want to play at that game. But life was a game of hide-and-seek, all right. He permitted himself the luxury of smiling as he once more looked over at the hammer-thrower and applauded Gee-gee. Odd, the idea of the hammer-thrower being that person he (Bob) was supposed to be, had never occurred to the latter! But no one ever would suspect that face! "My face is my fortune, sir," he might have said. The hammer-thrower caught Bob's smile.

"'Come and catch me,'" reiterated Gee-gee.

That might be applicable to the hammer-thrower. Bob, for the moment, felt as happy as a child who has discovered the solution of a puzzle. So that when Miss Gerald deigned casually to glance at him, she was surprised at his new expression. It seemed a long while since Bob had looked happy, but now he looked almost like his old self. Was it the near presence of the temperamental young thing that had wrought this change, Miss Gerald might well have asked herself.

Violet eyes looked now into temperamental dark ones. Gwendoline, too, was smiling—at the song. But it was that cryptic kind of a smile once more. Bob's smile was a rather large cryptic counterpart of Miss Gerald's. The temperamental little thing, though, didn't smile. She seemed reading Miss Gerald's soul. She was dropping a plumb-line deep down into it.

Then Miss Gerald turned again to the hammer-thrower, who talked to her just as if Bob hadn't seen anything, or imagined he had. Gee-gee sat down, at the same time condescending to bestow upon Bob a triumphal look. He had dared to scoff at her histrionic talent, had he? Well, she had shown him—and them. Maybe with a little publicity, she would become a star of dazzling magnitude. At that moment, the world looked bright to Gee-gee.

CHAPTER XVIII—A FORMIDABLE ADVERSARY

What a merry mad wag that hammer-thrower really must be at heart! thought Bob. How he was chuckling inside, or laughing in his sleeve most of the time while he went around with that heavy, serious, reliable visage of his! And that ponderous manner?—What lively little imps of mischief or fancy it concealed! That simulated slow tread, too?—Bob surmised he could get around pretty fast on occasions, if he wanted to, or had to. He was dancing very seriously with Miss Gerald now, seeming to take dancing as a kind of a moral lesson. Oh, that "duty talk" to Bob! He would "consider" Bob's case!—He wanted to ponder over it—he? And how painfully in earnest he had been when he had sprung what his father had said about not giving a fellow a shove when he was down!

Bob disentangled himself as soon as he could from the temperamental little thing and went into the billiard room, where he began to toy with the ivories. If there was one thing he could do, it was play billiards. But he retired to the seclusion of the billiard room now principally for the reason that he expected the hammer-thrower would follow him there. He felt almost sure the other would seek him. So, though Bob proceeded to execute one or two fancy shots with much skill, his thoughts were not on the ivories. He was considering his position in relation to the hammer-thrower. He (Bob) might entertain a profound conviction regarding the latter's profession, but could he prove anything?

True, he now remembered and could point out that the latter had attended all those functions where losses had occurred. But that wasn't in itself particularly significant. Other people, also, had attended all the functions in question. Bob couldn't even actually swear he had seen the other in his room when he had dropped something from Bob's window to some one lurking below. Bob hadn't had the chance to recognize him on that occasion. As far as evidence went, the "boot was all on the other leg." The hammer-thrower was obviously in a position to use Bob to pull chestnuts out of the fire for him.

But why had he not denounced Bob to the entire household, then and there, when he had discovered him before Gee-gee's door? Perhaps the hammer-thrower didn't yet know that any one knew there had been substituted one or two imitation articles of jewelry for real ones. If this were so, then from his point of view a denunciation of Bob might lead to an investigation which would reveal the fact that substitutions had occurred and in consequence he would be but curtailing the period of his own future activities in this decidedly fertile field. He hadn't, of course, refrained through any feeling of charity or commiseration for Bob. He had, moreover, paved the way to use Bob in the future, if need be, by discreetly mentioning the incident to Miss Gerald. Bob might prove serviceable as an emergency man. All this had no doubt been floating through the hammer-thrower's brain while he had stood there with that puzzled, aggrieved and righteous expression.

A slight sound behind him caused Bob to turn quickly and, as he had expected, he beheld the hammer-thrower. Here was renewed confirmation of that which he had just learned.

"I felt it my duty to inform Miss Gerald of what occurred last night," began the hammer-thrower without prelude.

"I know that already," said Bob, continuing his play.

"Ah, then I am wasting time. But having concluded that it was incumbent on me to take that course, I thought it but right to come to you and tell you what I had done. Square thing, you know."

Bob grinned. "Say it in Latin," he observed flippantly.

A slight frown gathered on the other's brow. "I really fail to understand. You placed me in an unpleasant position. It was not easy to speak of such a matter."

"Then why did you?" said Bob lightly, executing a difficult play.

"You do not seem to realize there are some things we have to do."

"Duty, eh?" observed Bob with another grin.

"Without wishing to pose as puritanical, or as a prig, I may say you have hit the nail fairly on the head."

"Oh, you aren't a prig," said Bob. "You're a lu-lu."

"I don't know whether you mean to be complimentary or not," returned the hammer-thrower with unvarying seriousness. "As I believe I have remarked before, you appear totally not to comprehend your own position. I might have awakened the house and what would have been your status then? There have of late been so many mysterious burglaries at large country-houses and in the big city homes of the affluent that a guest, found rambling about in pajamas at unseemly hours, courts, to put it mildly, suspicion. Anyhow, for my own protection, I had to speak to Miss Gerald. You see that, don't you? We'll waive the moral side."

"'Your own protection' is good," said Bob, sending his ball twice around the table and complacently observing the result.

"I mean that if it became known that I had secreted you in my room and said nothing about it, it would, in a measure, place me in the light of being an accomplice," returned the hammer-thrower, ignoring the point in Bob's last words. "I don't know whether anything will be discovered missing here or not, but if there should be—?"

"Things will be discovered missing, all right," returned Bob. "What was that you dropped out of the window in my room last night?"

The hammer-thrower stared at him. "I?—your room?" he said at length very slowly, with the most genuine amazement written all over his serious reliable features.

"You! My room!" repeated Bob. "You didn't expect me to come back. I gave you quite a surprise, didn't I? You are certainly some sprinter."

Still the hammer-thrower continued to stare. "Mad!" he said at last. "I hardly credited it before, but now—That private sanatorium!— No doubt, it was best."

Bob laughed. "That sanatorium fits in fine, doesn't it? You'll be trying the little abduction act next, yourself, I suppose."

"I'm trying to make up my mind whether you aren't really a dangerous person to be at large," said the hammer-man heavily. "You might say something like that to some one else. You appear absolutely irresponsible."

"I might," observed Bob tentatively. Oh, if he only could!

"However, I hardly think you will," remarked the other in his heaviest manner. "By the way, you play pretty good billiards."

"Thanks awfully. Want to play?"

"Don't mind." And the hammer-thrower took down a cue.

"I should dearly like to beat you," said Bob in wistful tones.

"And I should as dearly like not to be beaten by you, or any one else," returned the other.

"I know," conceded Bob, not without a touch of admiration, "you're a great chap for winning prizes and things. You've taken no end of cups, haven't you? I mean, legitimately."

"Yes; I usually go in to win." The other professed not to hear Bob's last words.

"And you've been feted some, in consequence, too, haven't you?" said Bob suddenly. "You were at the Duke of Somberland's, I remember." Meaningly. He remembered, too, that articles of great value had disappeared from the duke's place at the same time.

"I believe I was. Met no end of interesting people!"

"And weren't you at Lord Tumford's?" Bob recalled reading how jewels had mysteriously vanished in the case of Lord Tumford's guests, also.

"Yes, got asked over for the shooting. Believe I did very well for an American not accustomed to the British method of slaughter."

"No doubt," said Bob. The hammer-thrower was getting bigger in his way every moment. Now he had become an operator of international importance.

"Speaking about winning, you were on the losing team at college, weren't you?" he observed significantly.

"Quite so!" answered Bob. "We worked awfully hard and ought to have won, but fate, I guess, was against us."

"We," said the hammer-man in his ponderous way, "are fate. Arbiters of our destinies! We succeed, or we don't. And when we fail, it is we that fail. Fate hasn't anything to do with it."

"Maybe you're right," assented Bob. "I don't know. Anyhow, it's a test of true sportsmanship to know how to lose."

"Not to whine, you mean? True. But it's better not to lose. Now go ahead and try to beat me."

Bob tried his best. He let the other name the game and the number of points, and for a time it was nip and tuck. Once Bob ran a string of seventy. Then the hammer-thrower made one hundred and one. His playing was brilliant. Some of the heaviness seemed to have departed from his big frame. His steps nearly matched Bob's for litheness while his big fingers handled the cue almost daintily. All the inner force of the man seemed focused on the task of winning. He had made up his mind he couldn't lose. Bob was equally determined, too, not to lose.

The game seemed symbolical of that bigger game they were playing as adversaries, and more and more Bob realized here was an opponent not to be despised. He was resourceful, delicate, subtle, as he permitted Bob now to gaze behind that shield of heaviness. He had never before exhibited his real self at the table, playing heretofore in ponderous fashion, but this time, perhaps, he experienced a secret delight in tantalizing an enemy. Those big fingers seemed capable of administering a pretty hard squeeze when the hour arrived; they might even not hesitate at a death-clutch. The game now was very close.

"Shall we make it a thousand for the winner?" suggested the hammer-thrower.

"Haven't that much," said Bob. "Only got about seven dollars and a half, or so."

"I'll bet you seven dollars and a half, then."

Bob accepted, and immediately had a run of luck. He was within two points of being out. The hammer-thrower had about fifty to go.

"Get that seven dollars and a half ready," he said easily as he began his play.

"Maybe I shan't have to," replied Bob.

"Yes, you will." He spoke as one not capable of making mistakes about what he could do. And he didn't make a mistake this time. He ran out. Bob paid with as good grace as he could. Then the hammer-thrower moved heavily away and left Bob alone.

The latter didn't feel quite so jubilant now over his secret knowledge as he had a little earlier. The hammer-thrower had permitted him to test his mettle—indeed, he had deliberately put himself out to do so, and make Bob realize even more thoroughly that he might just about as well not know anything for all the good it would do him (Bob). His lips might as well be sealed, as far as his being able to prove anything; if he did speak, people would answer as the hammer-thrower had. "Mad!" Or worse! That sanatorium incident was certainly unfortunate.

Bob put his hand in his pocket to get his handkerchief to wipe a few drops of perspiration from his brow. He drew out his handkerchief, but he also drew out something else—something hard—that glittered-a ring—a beautiful one—with perfect blue white diamonds—a ring he remembered having seen on certain occasions adorning one of Miss Gerald's fingers.

Bob stared at it. He stood like one frozen to the spot. That hammer-man had done more than beat him at billiards. While he (Bob) had extended a portion of his person over the table to execute difficult shots the other had found it an easy trick to slip Miss Gerald's ring in the coat-tail pocket of Bob's garment. Could you exceed that for diabolical intention? Now what on earth was Bob to do with Miss Gerald's ring?

He couldn't keep it and yet he didn't want to throw away her property. It seemed as if he would be forced to, though. After an instant's hesitation he made up his mind that he would toss it out of the window and then write her anonymously where it could be found. The hammer-man hadn't calculated Bob would discover it on his person so soon, or perhaps he had told himself the odds were against Bob's discovering it at all. He would, of course, have preferred that others should discover it on Bob. The latter now strode to the window; the glittering ring seemed fairly to burn his fingers. He raised the curtain as softly as he could—the window was already open—and then suddenly started back.

The light from within, shining on the garden, revealed to him with disconcerting abruptness a man's face. The man sprang back with considerable celerity, but not before Bob had recognized in him that confounded maniac-medico. He had tracked Bob here, but not wishing to create a scene among Mrs. Ralston's guests, was no doubt waiting outside with his assistants and the first time Bob stepped out of the house, he expected to nab him. All the while Bob had been playing billiards, that miserable maniac-medico had probably been spying upon him, peeping from under the curtain.

Bob moved from the window, the ring still in his fingers, and at this inopportune moment, the monocle-man walked in. He seemed to have timed his coming to a nicety. Perhaps he had noticed that little episode at the window. Bob, in a panic, thrust the ring hurriedly into his waistcoat pocket and tried to face the other without showing undue agitation, but he feared guilt was written all over his countenance.

"Hot," muttered Bob. "Thought a breath of fresh air would do me good."

"Quite so. We English believe in plenty of fresh air," returned the monocle-man, just as if he swallowed the reason the other had given for going to the window.

But after that Bob couldn't get rid of him. It was as if he knew something was wrong and that Bob needed watching. He began to fool with the balls, telling how hard it was for him to get accustomed to these small American tables. The British game was far better, he went on, all the while keeping his eyes pretty closely on Bob, until the latter got desperate and went back to where people were. But the monocle-man went, too. By this time Bob was convinced the other knew what was in his pocket. "Caught with the goods!" That's the way the yellow press would describe his predicament.

"Aren't you the regular hermit-crab?" It was the temperamental little thing's reproachful voice that at this point broke in upon his sorrowful meditations, and Bob turned to her quickly. At the moment he was awfully glad she had come up. "What have you been doing?" she went on.

"Oh, just rolling the balls. Will you dance?" Eagerly.

"Can't! Engaged. You should have asked me sooner and not run away." Then perhaps she saw how disappointed Bob looked or caught that desperate expression in his eyes, for she added: "Yes, I will. Can say I was engaged to you first and forgot. Come on."

Bob did. He was a little afraid the monocle-man might not let him, but the other permitted him to dance. Perhaps he wouldn't have done so if he had known what was in Bob's mind. That young man felt as if he had now truly reached his last ditch.

"Say, I'm in an awful hole," he breathed to the temperamental little thing, as they glided over the floor.

"Are you?" She snuggled closer. "Anything worse than has been?"

"A heap worse! I've got something I simply must get rid of."

"What is it?" she said in a thrilling whisper.

"A ring." Hoarsely.

"No. Whose?"

"Miss Gerald's." More hoarsely still.

"How wildly exciting! Though I didn't think you would rob her." In an odd voice.

"I didn't."

"But you say you've got her ring?"

"Some one put it in my pocket."

"Isn't it the funny little hermit-crab, though!" she answered.

"Well, never mind whether you believe me or not. The point is, I've got to get rid of it and I can't. That monocle-man is watching me. I need help."

"Mine?" Snuggling once more.

"Yours. Will you do it?"

"Didn't I tell you I'd go through fire and water for you? Am I not now your eternal and everlasting chum? Say it."

"What?"

"That jolly-little-pal talk."

"Jolly little pal!" he breathed in her ear.

She sighed happily. "Now what do you want me to do?"

"I want you to take this ring"—slipping it into her fingers—"and return it to Miss Gerald's room. You can slip in without attracting any attention. Besides no one would think anything of your going in her room, even if you were seen doing so—you're such friends."

"But," she said wonderingly, "I don't see why you took it at all if—" She broke off—"Unless that monocle-man knows you've got it on you?"

"That's the point," observed Bob hoarsely.

"All right," she assented. "I'll do it. When?"

"Now."

"No," she said firmly. "Not until our dance is over. I want every bit of it. That's—that's my salary. My! I feel awful wicked with that ring in my hand. You can take a firmer hold of me if you want—the way you did that first day! I need reassuring!"

Bob laughed in spite of himself, but he reassured "jolly little pal," in the manner indicated.

"Now just fly around," she said.

And Bob "flew" with a recklessness that satisfied even her. When it was over she turned to him with an odd look.

"I've got another condition."

"What is it?"

"That you ask Miss Gerald to dance!"

"But—" he began, disconcerted as well as surprised.

"That's the condition."

"She would only refuse." Gloomily.

"Do you agree?" There was something almost wistful in the temperamental eyes of little pal at that moment.

"I—can't." Desperately.

"Very well. Take back the—"

"All right. I will," Bob half-groaned.

As he walked over toward Gwendoline Gerald, he saw the temperamental little thing moving toward the stairway. Half-way up, she stopped and looked back over the banister. Perhaps she wanted to see if Bob was fulfilling his part of the contract.

CHAPTER XIX—BOB FORGETS HIMSELF

"Miss Gerald," said Bob as formally as if he were quoting from one of those deportment books, "may I have the pleasure of this dance?"

Her reply was at variance with what "How to Behave in the Best Society" taught young ladies to say. "Why do you ask?" said Gwendoline Gerald quietly.

"Got to," said Bob.

"Why have you got to?"

"I promised I would."

"Who made you promise?"

Bob told.

"Do you have to do what she tells you?"

"In this instance."

"Of course you know what my reply will be?"

"I told her you would refuse."

"You would hardly expect me to dance with you after all I know about you, would you?" There was still that deadly quietness in her tones.

"All you think you know about me," Bob had the courage to correct her. "Of course not."

"Some one has taken one of my rings," observed Miss Gerald even more quietly.

"I haven't got it," exclaimed Bob. "Honest!" Wasn't he glad he had got rid of it?

The violet eyes studied Bob as if he were something strange and inanimate—an odd kind of a pebble or a shell. "You are sure?" said Miss Gwendoline.

"Positive," answered Bob in his most confident tones. He remembered now that during his dance with the jolly little pal he had observed the monocle-man talking with Miss Gerald. Perhaps he had told her he had seen the ring in Bob's fingers when the latter had gone to the window. The monocle-man might have been spying all the while, on the other side. There might have been two Peeping Toms interested in Bob's actions in the billiard room.

"Are you so positive you would be willing to submit to be searched?"

"I am that positive," Bob answered. And then went on more eagerly: "Maybe you haven't really lost it after all." He could say that and still tell the truth. "Why, it may be in your room now. You may find it on your table or your dresser when you go upstairs to retire."

Miss Gerald looked at him. "You seem to be rather certain?" she said tentatively.

"I am," said Bob. "I'd almost swear——" He stopped suddenly. It wouldn't do to be too certain.

"Don't you find your own words rather strange?" the girl asked.

"Everything's funny about me, nowadays," said Bob.

"Did you enjoy renewing your acquaintance with Miss ——?" She called Gee-gee by that other, more conventional name.

"I did not. I dislike her profoundly."

"Are you sure?" The violet eyes were almost meditative. "Now I should have thought——" She paused. Bob read the thought, however. A man like him was on a plane with Gee-gee; indeed, much lower. Miss Gerald would be finding in Gee-gee Bob's affinity next.

"You haven't refused me out-and-out, yet," he suggested. "To dance, I mean."

"You would rather, of course, I did refuse you?"

"Of course," Bob stammered. The mere thought of dancing with her once again as of yore gave him a sensation of exquisite pain. But naturally she would never dream of dancing with one she considered a—?

"Well, you may have the pleasure," she said mockingly.

Bob could not credit his hearing. She would permit him to touch her. Incredible! A great awe fell over him. He could not believe.

"I said you might have the pleasure," she repeated, accenting in the least the last word.

Bob caught that accent. Ah, she knew then, what exquisite pain it would be for him to dance with her! She was purposely punishing him; she wished to make him suffer. She would drive a gimlet in his heart and turn it around. Bob somehow got his arm about his divinity and found himself floating around the room, experiencing that dual sensation of being in heaven and in the other place at one and the same time.

It was a weird and wonderful dance. Through it all he kept looking down at her hair, though its brightness seemed to dazzle him. Miss Dolly had confided to Bob that he "guided divinely," but he didn't guide divinely now; he was too bewildered. Once he bumped his divinity into some one and this did not improve his mental condition. But she bore with him with deadly patience; she was bound to punish him thoroughly, it seemed.

Then that dual sensation in Bob's breast began gradually to partake more of heaven than of the other place, and he yielded to the pure and unadulterated joy of the divinity's propinquity. He forgot there was a big black blot on his escutcheon, or character. He ceased to remember he was a renegade and criminal. The nearness of the proud golden head set his heart singing until tempestuously and temerariously he flung three words at her, telepathically, from the throbbing depths of his soul.

The dance ending abruptly "brought him to." He looked around rather dazed; then struggling to awake, gazed at her. Her face still wore that expression of deadly calm and pride. Bob didn't understand. She was no statue, he would have sworn, yet now she looked one—for him. And a moment before she had seemed radiantly, gloriously alive—no Galatea before the awakening! It was as if she had felt all the vibrating joy of the dance. But that, of course, could not have been. Bob felt like rubbing his eyes when he regarded her. He did not understand unless—

She wished once more to "rub it in," to make him realize again more poignantly all that he had lost. She let him have a fuller glimpse of heaven just to hurl him from it. She liked to see him go plunging down into the dark voids of despair. He yielded entirely to that descending feeling now; he couldn't help it.

"I thank you," said Bob, in his best deportment-book manner.

The enigmatic violet eyes lighted as they rested on him. Bob would have sworn it was a cruel light. "Oh," she said, "as long as you are a guest—? There are certain formalities—"

"I understand," he returned.

The light in the violet eyes deepened and sparkled. So a cruel Roman lady might have regarded a gladiator in the arena, answering his appeal with "Thumbs down." Bob lifted his hand to his brow. The girl's proud lips—lips to dream of—were curved as in cruel disdain. Then Bob forgot himself again.

"I won't have you look at me like that," he said masterfully. "I'm not a criminal. Confound it, it's preposterous. I didn't steal your ring and I want you to know it, too. I never stole a thing in my life." They were standing somewhat apart, where they couldn't be overheard. He spoke in a low tone but with force, gazing boldly and unafraid now into the violet eyes.

"I won't let you think that of me," he said, stepping nearer. "Steal from you?" he scoffed. "Do you know the only thing I'd like to steal from you?" His eyes challenged hers; the violet eyes didn't shrink. "Yourself! I'd like to steal you, but hang your rings!" He didn't say "hang"; he used the other word. He forgot himself completely.

A garden of wild roses blossomed on the girl's fair cheek, but she held herself with rare composure. "I wonder, Mr. Bennett," she observed quietly, "how I should answer such mad irresponsible talk?"

"It's the truth. And if I were a thief—which I'm not—I wouldn't steal your rings. Even a thief wouldn't steal the rings of the girl he loves."

More roses! Outraged flushing, no doubt! Yet still the girl managed to maintain her composure. "You dare go very far, do you not, Mr. Bennett?"

"Yes; and I'll go further. I love every hair of your head. Even when you're cruel," he hurried on recklessly, "and heaven knows you can be cruel enough, I love you. I love your lips when they say the unkindest and most outrageous things to me. I love your eyes when they look scorn. I ought not to love you, but I do. Why, I loved you the first time I saw you. And do you think if I were all those things you think me, I'd dare stand up here and tell you that? I didn't mean to tell you ever that I loved you. But that's my answer when you imply I'm a rank criminal. A man's got to have a clear conscience to love you as I do. Such love can only go with a clear conscience. Why, you're so wonderful and beautiful to me I couldn't—" Bob paused. "Don't you see the point?" he appealed to her. "A man couldn't have you in his heart and not have the right to hold up his head among his fellow men."

Miss Gerald did not at once answer; she had not moved. The sweeping dark lashes were lowered; she was looking down. "You plead your cause very ingeniously, Mr. Bennett," she observed at length, her lashes suddenly uplifting. The lights were still there in the violet eyes; they seemed yet mocking him. "You invoke the sacred name of love as a proof of your innocence. The argument is unique if not logical," she went on with pitiless accents and the red lips that uttered the "sacred name of love" smiled. "I have been rather interested, however, in following your somewhat fantastic defense of yourself. That it has incidentally involved me is also mildly interesting. Do you expect me to feel flattered?" The red lips still smiled. Bob was quite near but she didn't move away. She seemed quite unafraid of him.

"You needn't feel ashamed," said Bob sturdily. And his eyes flashed. They seemed to say no woman ought to be ashamed of an honest man's love. "I may be mad over you," he went on, "but I'm not ashamed of it. There isn't a thought I have of you that doesn't make me want to be a better man, and a stronger and more useful one, too," he added, squaring his shoulders.

Again the long lashes swept slightly downward, masking the violet, and the girl's lips moved—a ripple of amusement, no doubt. She looked up, however, once more with that appearance of deadly calm. "Then you deny it, in toto, having seen my ring to-night?"

Bob swallowed. Again he dropped from the heights.

"You do not speak," said Miss Gerald, studying him.

"I—wish you wouldn't ask me that," he managed to say.

"Why not?" lifting her brows. "Even if you saw it you could say you hadn't."

"That's just the point," Miserably. "I couldn't."

"Then you did see it?"

"I did."

"You had it, perhaps?"

"I did."

"You have it now?"

"No."

"Ah, you have passed it on to an accomplice, perhaps." Mockingly. Miss Gerald drew up her proud figure. "And this is the man," she said, "who talks to me of love. Love!" With a low musical laugh. "The tenderest passion! The purest one! Dare you repeat now," with crushing triumph in the violet eyes, "what you said a moment ago."

"I love you," said Bob, with burning glance. "I shall carry your image with me to the grave."

This slightly staggered even one of her regal young bearing. His tone was that of the master once more. No criminal in his look when he said that! Miss Gerald's slender figure swayed in the least; her breast stirred. Bob put his handsome reckless face nearer. That was the way he answered her challenge. He wore his fighting look.

"I love you," he said. "And that," he flung at her, "is still the answer I dare make."

Miss Gerald did not reply to this bold defiance at once. How she would have answered, Bob never knew, for at that moment the hammer-thrower came up and the girl at once turned to him, looking slightly paler as she did so. Both then walked away, Bob's somber gaze following them. But he was not long permitted even this mournful privilege.

"Phone, sir," said a voice at his elbow. "Mr. Robert Bennett is urgently wanted on the phone."

"All right." And Bob followed the servant. "What now?" he asked himself wearily.

The voice at the other end was Dan's. Fortunately the telephone was isolated and no one in the house could catch what Bob said. The good old commodore frantically wished to know all about Gee-gee and Gid-up. He had heard that Bob had got out of the sanatorium and gone back to Mrs. Ralston's. Dan's desire for information was greater even than his resentment toward Bob, as he had stooped to calling him up.

Bob obliged the commodore with such news as he could give. He told how he had tried unsuccessfully to sway Gee-gee and to show her the error of her ways; how she, however, seemed resolutely determined on her course of action and was not to be swayed. He related also that there was a legal light in the house.

At this point Dan's remarks became explosive; it was like the Fourth of July at the other end of the line. Bob waited until the racket ceased and then he went on with further details, trying to be as conscientious and informing as possible. Finally he couldn't think of anything more to say. But Dan thought of a lot—and some of it was personal, too. It didn't ruffle Bob at all, however. It rolled off him like water off a duck's back.

"You'll be arrested," said Bob at last. "There's a law against that kind of talk through telephones, you know."

"I'm afraid it's all up," moaned Dan.

"'Fraid it is!" affirmed Bob. "How does Clarence take it?"

"He's sitting here, all broke up."

"Well, tell him to cheer up if he can," said Bob. "Gid-up isn't nearly so dangerous as Gee-gee. At least that's my opinion."

"Oh, isn't she?" sneered Dan. And then there was some more Fourth of July at the other end of the line.

Bob waited patiently for it to subside. "Is that all you wanted to talk with me about?" he asked at length.

"It is not," snapped Dan. "Those confounded blankety-blank detectives, some blankety-blank idiot has employed as gardeners about Mrs. Ralston's place, have arrested that-blankety-blank medical head of the private sanatorium."

"What?" exclaimed Bob jubilantly.

"They found him prowling around. He tells the police-station man who he is, but the police-station man won't believe him."

"Ha! ha!" Bob was glad he could laugh once more, but it was Fourth of July again for Dan.

"It isn't any blankety-blank laughing matter," he called back. "He's one of my witnesses and I don't want to lose him. Lost witnesses enough already!" Furiously.

"Well, why don't you get him out?" said Bob with a gratified snicker.

"I tried to, but that blankety-blank station-house man is a blank bullet-head and the blankety detectives insist he shall be held, as they saw him looking through a window. What I want you to do is to come down to the village and help get him out."

"Me?" said Bob loftily. "Me help get him out?"

"Yes, you can acknowledge he was after you, an escaped patient."

"Where is he now?" asked Bob.

"Cell."

"Well, you tell the station-man for me that he had better put him in a padded room. Ha! ha!" And Bob hung up the receiver.

But almost immediately the bell rang again.

"Hello!" said a voice. It was the telephone operator. "Is Mr. Bennett still there? Oh! Well, there's a party on the long distance wants to speak to you."

"Hello; that you, Bob?" came in far-away accents.

"It's me. Who are you?"

"Dad."

"Oh, hello, dad!" Bob tried to make his voice joyful.

"I called you up to tell you I caught a fifty-seven pounder. Thought you'd like to congratulate me."

Bob did.

"They've made me a member of the Pius Piscatorials—swell club down here," continued dad jubilantly, and again Bob did the congratulating act. "By the way, how's hustling?" went on dad.

"I'm hustling all right."

"That's good. Well, good-by, son. I'll be short of funds presently, but that doesn't worry me. I'm having the time of my life. By-by, dear boy."

"By-by, dad, dear."

"Hold on, Mr. Bennett." It was the telephone operator once more. "There's another party that's bound to speak to you, and take it from me I don't like the sound of his voice. I hope he isn't like that first party that was talking to you. What us poor girls has to put up with is something shameful, and—All right. Go ahead."

"This is Dickie," said a voice. "Say! you leave my girl alone. I've heard of your goings-on."

"Who told you?" asked Bob. "That Peeping Tom? That maniac-medico?"

"I told you before I was going to marry her. You keep off the premises if you know what is good for you." Dickie was so mad he was childish.

"No, you're not going to marry her," said Bob.

"You—you don't mean to say you're engaged to her?" came back in choked tones.

"No. She's only my jolly little pal. But she thinks a lot of what I tell her and I'll pick out a real man for her some day. You aren't good enough. A chap that will punch another chap when he can't defend himself isn't the chap for jolly little pal."

"I didn't punch you when you couldn't defend yourself," said Dickie indignantly.

"I'm the one to know. You gave it to me all right, and thereby settled your chances with her. Do you think I'd let a girl like her marry a chap like you? Why, you might come home and beat your wife! You're capable of it. I refuse my consent absolutely. I shall advise her to have nothing whatever to do with you."

Dickie couldn't speak and Bob left him in a state of coma. This time Bob was suffered to leave the telephone booth. He was awfully glad they had the maniac-medico locked up. Maybe he would get a cute little room with a cunning little window, and maybe there'd be a landscape? But there wouldn't be any flowers.

Just at this moment the temperamental little thing hurried up to Bob in a state of great agitation. He saw that something serious had happened.

CHAPTER XX—HAND-READING

"Did you get rid of it?" he asked hurriedly.

"I did not," she gasped. "That mean old monocle-man wouldn't let me. He's just kept his eye on me every moment. When I went upstairs, he followed. There he is now. See how he's watching us. Oh, what shall I do, if they find me with it?"

"Give it to me," said Bob.

"No, I won't."

"But do you realize what it means if they find it on you?" he asked in alarm.

"We would go to jail together," said jolly little pal.

"But I won't have you go to jail. It's preposterous."

"Maybe I deserve it," she remarked, "for having 'peached.' I hope," wistfully, "our cells will be close together. Did you have a nice dance with Miss Gerald?"

"Give it to me," commanded Bob sternly. "If you don't, I'll—I'll take it from you."

But she put her hand behind her. "Isn't Gwendoline the most beautiful thing in the world?" she said. "We'll talk about her in jail. It'll help pass the time."

"Give—"

"I'm not the least bit jealous, because now I'm only your really-truly little pal," she went on. "I wish I could be your best man. But I don't suppose that's feasible."

"Give—"

"I might swallow it," she observed tentatively.

"Great heavens!" he reached for her hand.

"Aw!—fortune-telling?" said a voice.

"Yes; he was just going to read my palm," answered jolly little pal promptly while Bob turned rather nervously to regard the monocle-man.

"Perhaps—aw!—I could read it," suggested the monocle-man, looking at the closed fingers. "I have some—aw!—skill that way. Perhaps, Miss Dolly—aw!—you would permit me to look at your heart line?"

"I just won't," said Miss Dolly, with flashing eyes.

Bob watched her closely. If she tried to swallow it, he would stop her.

"How—aw!—very unkind!" said the monocle-man. "If you would—aw!—permit me, I could tell you—? aw!—just what kind of a man you're going to marry."

"I'm not going to marry any one," replied the jolly little pal.

"Please now, do—aw!" he urged.

"Well, if you want to be tiresome." She gave him the hand that didn't hold the ring.

"Impulsive! Charming!" he said, bending his monocle owlishly over the soft pink palm. "Now the other?"

"Won't!" she returned succinctly.

Bob drew yet nearer. He believed she was quite capable of carrying out that threat of swallowing it.

"But how can I complete telling your fortune—aw!—unless I see the other hand?" expostulated the monocle-man with a pleasant smile. "I desire especially to examine the Mount of Venus."

"There isn't any mountain any more," said the jolly little pal. "It's been moved away."

"Aw! How interesting! Then we might survey the vale of friendship."

She looked around like a bird in a snare; the hammer-man was not far away and impulsively she flew over to him.

"Was this our dance? I'm so forgetful!"

"It wasn't, but it is," he returned with a smile. Obviously he was flattered. Heretofore Miss Dolly had not acted particularly prepossessed by the hammer-thrower; he hadn't any temperament—so she thought; he didn't swing one around with enough abandon. He was one of those serious goody-goody dancers. He swung Miss Dolly very seriously now; they went so slowly for her that once she stumbled over his feet. It was evident their temperaments didn't match. Or maybe what she held in one hand had made her terribly self-conscious. Bob watched them gloomily. He feared she might swallow it during the dance, but she didn't, for the little hand was partly closed still when she left the hammer-thrower and Bob gazed around for that confounded monocle-man. The latter, however, had apparently lost interest in palm-reading and the temperamental little thing, for he was nowhere to be seen. Miss Dolly's eyes were at once frightened and strange when she fluttered again to Bob's side.

"Oh, I've done the most awful thing," she confided quite breathlessly to him.

"You—you haven't swallowed it?" he exclaimed in alarm. He thought he had watched her closely, but still she might have found opportunity—she might have made a swift movement to her lips which he had failed to observe.

"No, I haven't swallowed it," she answered. "I've done worse."

"Worse? What could be worse?"

"I slipped it into his waistcoat pocket."

"Whose? The hammer-thrower? No? By jove!—"

"I did it when I tripped. And I tripped purposely, and when he was very gallant and kept me from falling, I—I slipped it in. And isn't it awful? Poor man! He's such a goody-good. You don't mind, do you?" Anxiously.

"Oh, I mind a heap," said Bob jovially. "Ho! ho!"

"I was afraid you might scold."

"Scold? No, indeed. I'm awfully obliged and I only wish I could do something for you to show how thankful I am."

"Do you? Then you might—" She gazed toward the conservatory where it was dim and shadowy. "No; it wouldn't do. We're not engaged any more. Besides—" And she looked toward a straight proud figure with golden hair. She didn't finish what she was going to say. Only—"I guess I won't make you," she added.

"Thanks," said Bob. "You're sure the best pal a chap ever had. But honest! I hate to be mean and disappoint you after all you've done. And I might volunteer, if you'd make it just one—or, at the most, two."

A moment the temperamental little thing seemed to waver. Then the rosebud lips set more firmly. "No," she said. "It's awfully dear of you to offer, but I don't want any. You've made me see the error of my ways. I've reformed. I only want to be your jolly little pal. But you haven't any conscientious scruples about the way I disposed of it, have you?" she asked, swiftly changing the subject.

"Conscientious scruples? Not one. Ho! ho!"

But the laughter faded suddenly from Bob's lips. At that moment the hammer-thrower chanced to put his fingers in his waistcoat pocket. Then he gave a slight start and glanced toward the temperamental little thing; his brow was lowering, and he appeared to meditate. Bob knew there must be murder in his heart. Just then from across the room, Bob saw the monocle-man approaching the hammer-thrower.

The latter cast a swift look toward him of the monocle. It was the look of a man who for the first time, perhaps, fully realizes, or begins to realize certain unexpected forces arrayed against him. He now had the ring and he dared not keep it. If he had never entertained any suspicions regarding the monocle-man's identity before, there was something about the other now that awoke sudden and secret misgivings. The monocle-man didn't make much of a point of disguising his watchfulness at the present time. That was odd—unless he didn't greatly care just now whether any one guessed his identity or not. Possibly the psychological moment was approaching.

The hammer-thrower thought, no doubt, that Bob had told the temperamental little thing that he (the hammer-man) had taken the ring from Miss Gerald's room and Miss Dolly had offered to return it to the hammer-thrower. And she had found a way to do so. It was clever. But the hammer-thrower was not in a mood to appreciate the grim jest. Now that the tables were turned, Bob and Miss Dolly would make it their business to see that the glittering trifle was found in *his* possession. The hammer-thrower couldn't dispose of it under the circumstances; he was in exactly the same predicament Bob had been in. Suddenly he seemed to make up his mind what to do; he adopted the most daring expedient. In those few moments he had done some very rapid thinking. He stepped toward Miss Gerald now, his face wearing its most reliable expression. Honesty fairly radiated from his square solid countenance.

"Miss Gerald," he said, "may I speak with you privately?"

"Is it important?" she asked.

"Very!" in his most serious manner.

She complied with his request, and they withdrew from the hearing of others.

"Miss Gerald," he began abruptly, "have you lost a ring?"

She gazed at him in surprise.

"I have."

"Is this it? I believe I recognize it as one you have worn."

"It is." Gwendoline's look swerved toward Bob. "But—" she began.

"You do not understand how it came in my possession?" he asked, in an even monotonous tone.

"I certainly did not think that you—"

"You didn't think I had it?" Seriously.

"I did not." And again she looked toward Bob.

"I did not know I had it myself," he observed gravely, "until just this minute. You believe me, I trust?"

"Yes," she said slowly, "I believe you. But how—?" Again she paused.

"Did I come by it? A certain young lady I danced with just now placed it in my waistcoat pocket."

The hammer-thrower held himself squarely, with a poise that expressed rectitude. He was rather well satisfied with what he had done. He argued that his action, from Miss Gerald's point of view, must be that of an innocent man. If he (the hammer-thrower) had taken the ring it wasn't likely he would step up to Miss Gerald and offer it back to her. His bold move complicated the issue; but he did not doubt, however, that he would emerge from the affair with credit.

"Of course I am aware that it is a serious charge to make," went on the hammer-thrower, "but what was I to do? I never was put in a more painful position."

"Painful, indeed," replied Miss Gerald sympathetically. "Of course it was a joke."

"I am glad you take that view of it," he replied. "You can see that naturally I found it deucedly awkward. Things have been disappearing in so many country-houses, don't you know. It wouldn't have been a joke for me if I hadn't fortunately discovered it as I did. Under the circumstances, I don't really appreciate Miss Dolly's jokes."

"But mightn't it have been some one else?" suggested Gwendoline.

"I danced only with you and Miss Dolly."

"Well, naturally, it wouldn't be I," said Gwendoline with a smile. "There's Dolly now talking with Mr. Bennett and Lord Stanfield, Suppose we speak to her. But I wouldn't have any one else know for the world. I'm really very sorry Dolly's heedlessness should have caused one of my aunt's guests any embarrassment." Miss Gerald was graciousness itself.

In spite of the thrill of the moment, the hammer-thrower couldn't prevent an expression of honest approval gleaming from his eyes. "You are very kind," he said in a low tone. "You will never know all this visit has meant to me. I, too, regret exceedingly that what you regard as one of Miss Dolly's mad pranks—and we all know how prone she is to do the unconventional—should have involved me in a little episode that, perhaps, isn't so agreeable as it should be. I trust, though, you don't blame me for coming to you at once about the matter?"

"Why should I blame you?" The violet eyes full on the deep serious ones.

"I suppose I might just have placed it somewhere, on the mantle, for example, and not said anything about Miss Dolly's part in the affair," he observed musingly. "It might have been more chivalrous. One doesn't like to complain of a woman, you know, and a fellow guest at that." With regret that sounded genuine.

"I think you took the only course a conscientious man could," said Gwendoline Gerald. "Indeed, I can appreciate your position. You did what any honest man would feel impelled to do."

Again that gracious smile! Again a slight gleaming in the hammer-man's eyes! At the moment she seemed to realize in every way the poet's picture of regal young womanhood—"divinely tall" and most divinely fashioned, she appeared, as she stood with the light from a great chandelier full upon her.

"Your approval is very dear to me," the hammer-thrower murmured. "I think I have your friendship. That is much—much, indeed. But—" For a moment he seemed about to say more. His strong, honest-looking face surely wore an expression of some feeling deeper than friendship.

Would Gwendoline Gerald have shrunk from a verbal expression of what his look seemed to imply? The violet eyes never appeared deeper, more enigmatic—receptive. The hammer-thrower did not go on, however. He reverted to that other topic.

"Perhaps it would be as well to drop the matter altogether," he remarked. "I am quite satisfied to do so, if you are."

"That is nice of you," she said in a tone that implied she still approved of him. "But I think I shall speak to Dolly. Or, at least, let her see the ring is on my finger."

"I can't understand why she should have done it," he observed in puzzled accents as they crossed the room. "I can't quite see how it can be classed as a joke."

"Dolly has the wildest idea of humor," returned Gwendoline. "As a little girl she was always doing the maddest things. Perhaps, too, she has been reading about those sensational robberies and wished to perpetrate a hoax."

"I say, that would have been rather rough on a fellow, wouldn't it?"

"And then, after creating a little excitement, she would have come forward and said she did it. Maybe she read about that escapade of young men and girls at an English house-party. They carried off valuables in an automobile, and returned the same, piece-meal, by parcel post. I don't say my explanation of Dolly's prank is a correct one," said Miss Gerald, tentatively lifting long sweeping lashes to regard her companion, "but it may in some measure throw light upon it."

"Unless—?" He paused.

"Unless what?" she asked.

"Nothing. Only I was thinking—"

The violet eyes became suddenly darker. "You mean about what you told me this morning—about Mr. Bennett and how you found him—?"

"I really didn't wish to speak of that, only it was strange—" He stopped.

"Strange, indeed," she observed, studying him.

"Anyhow, I can't see how to connect that with this," he confessed.

"There does seem a missing-link somewhere," observed the girl. "Do you"—and her eyes were again full upon the deep serious ones—"like Mr. Bennett?"

"I neither like nor dislike him." They had stopped for a moment in a doorway. "His manners have been rather extraordinary. I honestly can't make him out. He looks rational enough and yet he acts most irrationally."

"I am going to tell you a great secret," said the girl. "Please do not speak of it to any one else. Some one in the house has been taking things—in earnest, I mean."

"No? Is it possible?" he observed. "Then it wouldn't have been nice for me if that ring—?" Honest indignation shone from his eyes. "I must say Miss Dolly did take a confounded liberty."

"Under the circumstances, yes," said the girl gravely.

"You say things are missing? Great Scott!"

"I did not say missing." Quickly. "It is a case of substitution."

"Pardon me if I fail to understand."

She explained. "By jove! that is clever. I am honored by your confidence. I won't betray it. Your aunt is naturally distressed?"

"Naturally—though she appears the same as usual. However, she is determined to put an end to these affairs. Society has been frightfully annoyed. It is not nice to ask some one down and then to have her lose—"

"I understand," said the hammer-thrower gravely. "If your aunt can stop these unfortunate occurrences society will owe her a great debt. But tell me further, if I am not intruding too greatly on your confidences, does the finger of suspicion point anywhere?"

"Yes," returned the girl.

"Of course," he said, and looked toward Bob.

That young man's face did not now express any trace of satisfaction or jovial feeling. He looked both puzzled and worried, and glanced apprehensively from time to time at the sentimental young thing. The monocle-man *was* telling her fortune now. With British persistence he had reverted to the subject upon again approaching the couple, which he did almost immediately after the hammer-thrower returned to Miss Gerald her ring.

"You missed your ring?" said the hammer-thrower after a pause.

"Yes. But I never imagined—"

"It would be returned in such an extraordinary manner? I don't see where he—?" And the hammer-man paused again with downbent brows.

It was not hard for her to read the thought. He did not see just where Bob Bennett "came in." That's what he once more implied. He didn't wish to be unjust to any one. His expression said that.

"I guess it must just have been a whim," he conceded after a moment, handsomely. "After all, it's proofs that count." The sentence had a familiar sound to Miss Gerald who entertained a vague impression she had said something like it to Bob. They approached Dolly.

CHAPTER XXI—HEART OF STONE

"Did he tell you that I—?" began Miss Dolly at once, and snatching her arm from that tiresome monocle-man.

"Yes, my dear," said Gwendoline. "And he seemed a little hurt at your sense of humor."

The temperamental little thing stood like a wild creature at bay, her eyes glowing like those of a fawn about to receive the arrow of a hunter or a huntress. Miss Gerald did not look a very remorseless huntress, however.

"How did he know I did it?" said Dolly with a glance toward the hammer-thrower. "He didn't catch me at it." Defiantly.

"Deduction, my dear," replied Gwendoline.

"He can't prove it. I defy him." The jolly little pal felt now how one feels when he or she is haled into a court of justice. She wouldn't "peach" though. They could put her through the third or the thirty-third degree and she wouldn't tell on Bob. Never! "You have only *his* word," with another glance at the hammer-thrower, "and maybe my word is as good as his." She had to tell a whopper; but she would tell a million for Bob. It was a pal's duty to.

"But I saw you do it," now interposed the monocle-man with a quiet smile.

She almost wilted at that, then threw back her head farther.

"I"—Bob stepped quickly forward—"gave it to her. It was I," gravely to Miss Gerald, "who had your ring. Think what you please." She had already passed judgment on him, he remembered.

"Don't you believe him," tempestuously interrupted the temperamental little thing. "I took it myself. It—it was just a joke."

"That's what Miss Gerald and I were saying just now," observed the hammer-thrower heavily. He held himself just as if he were a remote, rather puzzled bystander.

Bob gave a hoarse laugh. He couldn't control himself.

"I beg your pardon," observed the monocle-man, "but I am afraid Miss Dolly, in her zeal, is rather misleading in her statements. Her vale of friendship, I have noticed, on her palm, is well developed. At the same time I can not let her wrongfully accuse herself, even though the matter should pass as a jest. I have to tell the truth—you must forgive me, Miss Dolly. But I saw Mr. Bennett pass you that ring during the dance."

"But why should he?" spoke up Miss Gerald. "Can't you enlighten me, dear?" To the temperamental young thing.

"I won't say a word," said the latter at a loss. "Only I'd like to tell you"—to the monocle-man—"how much I like you."

"I'm sorry to have displeased you," he answered simply. "You have really a charming hand. As for the reason you ask"—to Miss Gerald—"it should not be difficult to find. I conclude that Mr. Bennett asked Miss Dolly to return the ring to Miss Gerald's room. I think that was what she was trying to do and I'm afraid I prevented her."

"But why should Mr. Bennett"—Gwendoline did not deign to address that young man direct—"have asked Dolly to do that?"

"Maybe," suggested the monocle-man, "Mr. Bennett will answer that himself."

"What's the use?" said Bob. "Nobody believes anything I say." Miss Gwendoline still acted as if she did not see him.

"If you take him to jail, I'm going too," remarked the temperamental little thing. "If he's guilty, I—"

"You suggest, then, he is guilty?" said the monocle-man quickly.

"No; no! I—"

"I fear you have suggested it," he interrupted pointedly.

"If people confess do they get lighter sentences?" she asked with a quick breath.

"Usually," said the monocle-man.

Jolly little pal pondered painfully. Perhaps she saw plainer than Bob how clear was the case against him. "Why don't you?" she suggested.

Bob smiled feebly. "The answer I make is the same one I gave to Miss Gerald when I last spoke to her."

A flame sprang to Gwendoline's cheek.

"You dare say that now—with all this evidence against you?" She showed herself keenly aware of his presence now.

"I dare." He stepped to her side and looked into her eyes. "My eyes are saying it now."

The girl's breast stirred quickly. Did she fear he would say those words aloud, before all the others? He was reckless enough to do so.

"Do you understand or shall I make it plainer?" he asked, swinging back his blond head.

"I do not think that will be necessary," she answered with some difficulty.

"What *is* it all about?" said the hammer-man, and there was a slight frown on his brow.

"You ought to know," returned Bob, as his eyes met swiftly the other's. For a moment gaze encountered gaze. Bob's now was sardonically ironical, yet challenging. The hammer-thrower's was mystified. Then the latter shrugged.

"Is he mad as well as a—" he spoke musingly.

"Thief," said Bob. "Say it right out. I'm not afraid of the word."

The hammer-thrower sighed heavily. "What are we to do?" he said to Miss Gerald sympathetically. "It is needless to say, you can command me."

"Isn't that lovely?" Sotto voce from Bob.

"I'm terribly afraid the affair has passed from the joke stage," said Gwendoline Gerald and once more she appeared cool and composed. Again she made Bob feel he was but a matter for consideration—an intrusive and unwelcome matter that had to be disposed of. "What ought I to do?"

"Arrest me, of course," returned Bob. "I've been waiting for it for some time. And the funny part is, the affair hasn't passed from the joke stage. You know that." To the hammer-man. "Why don't you chuckle?"

"I suppose I may as well tell you I'm a bogus lord," unexpectedly interrupted the monocle-man at this moment. "My name is not even a high-sounding one." The hammer-thrower started slightly. "It's plain Michael Moriarity. But I was once a lord's valet." He had dropped his drawl, though he still kept his monocle. "I am sorry to have intruded as a real personage among you all, although there are plenty of bogus lords floating through society."

"Oh, you didn't deceive me," answered jolly little pal. "I knew who you were."

"Well, you certainly hoodwinked the rest of us," observed the hammer-thrower slowly. He stood with his head down as if thinking deeply. When he looked up, he gazed straight into the monocle-man's eyes. They were twinkling and good-humored. An arrest in high society was rather a ceremonious affair. You didn't take a man by the scruff of the neck and yank him to the patrol wagon. There were polite formalities to be observed. The end had to be accomplished without shocking or disturbing the other guests. The truly artistic method would, in fact, be the attainment of the result while the guests remained in absolute ignorance, for the time being, of what had been done.

"I'm afraid I've got to do my duty," observed the monocle-man to Bob. "You look like a man who would play the game. A game loser, I mean?" Suggestively.

"Oh, I'm a loser all right," said Bob, looking at the hammer-man. For a moment he wondered if he should speak further. He could imagine how his words would be received. He didn't forget that he hadn't a shadow of proof against the hammer-man. Miss Gerald would think he was accusing an innocent person and she would despise him (Bob) only the more—if that were possible. To speak would be but to court the contempt of the others, the laughter of the hammer-man. Bob's thoughts were terribly confused but he realized he might as well remain silent; indeed, perhaps it would be better for the present.

"Anyhow, what I told you wasn't so," said jolly little pal to the monocle-man. "And I repeat I will never testify to it." She was awfully dejected.

"Yes, you will," said Bob monotonously. "As I told you, I won't let you get into trouble."

"Besides there's all that other evidence," suggested the monocle-man.

"I can explain that away," returned Bob. Then he thought: Could he? Would Dan and Clarence stand by him now and acknowledge it was they he had let out of the house at that unseemly hour? He doubted it. Dickie, too, wouldn't be very friendly. Their last conversation over the telephone was far from reassuring. "No; I am not sure that I can," Bob added. He still had to remember he was the impersonation of Truth.

"You refer to Miss Gerald's having seen you wandering about the house after the others had retired, I presume?" suggested the monocle-man, who was enjoying the conversation immensely. It was the kind of a situation he liked. He wouldn't have curtailed it for the world. When the hammer-man heard the question, his brows lifted slightly. Surely a momentary glint of gladness or satisfaction shone from his gaze. But it receded at once. He listened attentively.

"Yes, I was referring to that," answered Bob, gazing at Gwendoline. She, condemn him to a prison cell! She, swear away his liberty! He gazed wistfully, almost sadly at the sweet inexorable lips which might ruin his life. He didn't feel resentful; he only determined to put up the best fight he could when the time came.

"Is—is it necessary to proceed to extremities?" said the hammer-man at this point sedulously. "Would not the mere fact that we all know about the matter be sufficient punishment?" He appealed to Miss Gerald. "My father used to tell me that when a man was down, if we could see the way to extend a helping hand, we would be doing the right thing. I think the world is becoming more tolerant and there is a tendency to give a person a chance to reform, instead of locking him up."

Again Bob laughed. In spite of his unhappiness and that weight of melancholy, the other's heavy humor tickled Bob's funny bone. Think of the hammer-man pretending to try to keep Bob out of jail! Didn't he know how to play his cards? The deadly joke was on Bob.

"Don't appeal too hard in my behalf, old chap; you might strain yourself," he said to the hammer-thrower.

But the hammer-thrower pretended not to hear. He kept his sedulous, humane glance on Miss Gerald.

"You mean you would have my aunt take no action in the matter?" she said, and the lovely face was now calm and thoughtful.

"Please do!" This from jolly little pal. "Dear, dear Gwendoline! It'll be such a favor to me. And I'll love you dearly."

"You certainly are a very doughty champion of Mr. Bennett, Dolly," observed Miss Gerald. There was a question in her look and her words might have implied that Bob had been making love to the temperamental little thing, even when he dared tell Miss Gerald he cared for her. Gwendoline's face wore an odd smile now.

"I'm not interested for the reason you think," answered the temperamental little thing spiritedly. "He never made love to me— real love. I tried to make him, because he is all that should appeal to any woman, but he wouldn't," she went on tempestuously, regardlessly. "And then we vowed we'd be pals and we are. And I'll stand by him to the last ditch."

"You are very loyal, dear," said Gwendoline quietly.

"Besides, he's in love with some one else," she shot back, and Bob shifted. There was a directness about jolly little pal that was sometimes disconcerting.

The hammer-man looked quickly toward Miss Gerald, and his eyes were full of jealousy for an instant. He was not sorry that Bob was going to "get his." Nevertheless, he would plead for him again, he wouldn't cease to be consistent in his role.

"I'll tell you who it is, too, if you want to know," the temperamental little thing went on to Gwendoline.

"My dear, I haven't asked. It seems to me," coldly, "we are slightly drifting from the subject."

"I believe you stated just now that you and Mr. Bennett vowed to be pals," interposed the monocle-man regarding Miss Dolly. "Does that mean you agreed to be accomplices—to divide the 'swag,' in the parlance of the lower world?" The monocle-man was enjoying himself more and more. He was finding new interest in the scene. It was more "meaty" than he had dared hope.

"She doesn't mean anything of the kind," put in Bob savagely. "She just extended the hand of friendship. She's a good fellow, that is all, and I won't have you imply the slightest thing against her. You understand that, Mr. Bogus Lord?"

"I only asked a question," observed the monocle-man humbly.

"Well, you've got the answer." In the same aggressive manner. "She's a—a brick and I won't have any harm come to her on my account."

"None of us would have any harm come to Dolly," said Gwendoline coldly.

"I wanted him to elope with me, but he wouldn't," went on the temperamental little thing, thinking fast. Bob listened in despair. "I didn't know then it was only friendship I felt. I thought it was love. And when he refused, I was furious. To be revenged, I went to that horrid man"—looking at him of the monocle—"and told him a pack of lies."

"Lies?" said the monocle-man, smiling sweetly and screwing his glass in farther.

"Yes, and that's the reason I shall give on the witness-stand." Defiantly. "I'll tell the truth there—let every one know how horrid and wicked I was."

The monocle-man shook his head with mild disapproval. "What do you say to that, Mr. Bennett?" he asked softly.

"Of course I can't let her do anything to incriminate herself," answered Bob mournfully. "To prevent her doing so I shall have to avow right now—? and I do"—firmly—"that those were not lies, but truths she told you."

"Please!—please!—" said jolly little pal piteously.

"Truths!" said Bob again boldly.

Miss Dolly gave a great sigh. "Are you going to confess you are guilty of all they charge?"

"I am not." Stubbornly. "I am not guilty."

"I'm rather afraid certain evidence, including Miss Dolly's truths, which you acknowledge as such, might tend to show you are," suggested the monocle-man.

Again Miss Dolly thought fast. Bob wouldn't let her declare her accusations of him lies; therefore only one alternative remained.

"*I* have a confession to make," she said solemnly.

Bob looked startled. "Don't!—" he began. He wondered into what new realm her inventive faculties would lead her.

Page

"Mr. Bennett," observed the monocle-man gravely, "I have to remind you that anything you say can be used against you. And your manner now, in seeking to restrain or interfere with what Miss Dolly has to say, will certainly hurt your case."

Bob groaned. He cast hunted eyes upon Miss Dolly. The jolly little pal breathed hard, but there was a look of determination in the dark soulful eyes.

"Mr. Mike Something, or whatever your name is," she said to the monocle-man in a low tense tone, "I am all that which you suggested."

He overlooked the scornful mode of address. He rubbed his hands softly; his eyes were pleased. "You mean about agreeing to be accomplices and to divide the 'swag'?"

"Yes." Fatalistically.

Bob groaned again.

The temperamental little thing looked up in the air. She would be mainly responsible for sending Bob to jail—the thought burned. What was a treacherous but repentant pal's duty under the circumstances? She had a vision, too, of those adjoining cells.

"You see," she began dreamily, "my father is rather sparing of the spending money he allows me, and I have terribly extravagant tastes. Why, my hats alone cost a fortune. I simply have got to have nice and expensive things." Again Bob groaned. Dolly dreamed on: "I've bushel-baskets of silk stockings, for example. See!" Displaying an exquisite ankle. "My gowns all come from Paris. Gwendoline can tell you that." Miss Gerald did not deny. "And they're not gowns from those side-street dressmakers, either. They come from *the* places on the rue de la Paix. Besides"—Dolly's dream expanded—"I like to take things." Another groan from Bob. "I think I'm a clepto."

"There isn't one word of truth in what she's saying," exclaimed Bob indignantly. "Why, it's outrageous. She doesn't realize what she's doing."

"Yes, I do," returned little pal with a stanch and loyal glance. "Why should you take all the blame when I'm entitled to half of it?"

"You aren't entitled to any of it," he retorted helplessly. "And there isn't any blame for you to share, either."

"Do you expect us to believe that?" observed the monocle-man reproachfully.

"No, I don't."

"Or a jury?"

"Perhaps not."

"Really, old chap"—began the hammer-man sedulously, and he looked awfully sorry. Perhaps he was going to extend his sympathy.

"Say it in Latin!" interrupted Bob ungratefully.

"What does he mean?" queried the monocle-man.

"I'm really at a loss," answered the hammer-thrower.

That gentleman had gleaned a great deal of information of a most gratifying nature. He didn't know all the whys and wherefores, but it was sufficient that Bob seemed too deep in the toils to extricate himself. A happy (to the hammer-man) combination of circumstances had involved the other.

"Please let him go," again pleaded Miss Dolly to Gwendoline. "Be a dear. Besides, think how he—" She went over to Miss Gerald suddenly and whispered two words—two ardent electrical words!

Gwendoline's eyes flashed but she did not answer. One of the hammer-thrower's hands closed.

"I fear Miss Gerald couldn't do that now, if she wanted to," interposed the monocle-man. "It isn't altogether her affair or her aunt's. You see, there are other people who gave those other social functions Mr. Bennett attended. They may not incline to be sentimentally—I may say foolishly lenient. So you see even if I desired to oblige a lady"—bowing to Dolly "whom I esteem very much, my hands are tied. Justice, in other words, must take its course."

Bob looked at Gwendoline. "Some day, Miss Gerald, you may realize you helped, or tried to help, convict an innocent man."

"She doesn't care," said the temperamental little thing vehemently. "She's got a stone for a heart." Only that cryptic smile on the proud beautiful lips answered this outbreak. The jolly little pal went right over to her again. "Anyhow," she said, "he kissed me."

Just for an instant Miss Gerald's sweeping lashes lifted to Bob. Just for an instant, too, Miss Gerald's white teeth buried themselves in that proud red upper lip. Miss Dolly turned to the monocle-man. "Now, I'm ready to go with you," she said.

"Oh, I don't want you"—then he added "yet! You will appreciate, Mr. Bennett"—turning to Bob—"that the more quietly—I want to show you all the consideration possible—"

"I'll go quietly," muttered Bob. "No use raising a row! I'll go like a gentleman. I'll make myself as little obnoxious and objectionable to the rest of Mrs. Ralston's guests as possible." Bitterly. "Good-by, Miss Gerald." That young lady didn't answer. "Won't you say good-by?" repeated Bob. There was a gleam of great pleasure in the hammer-thrower's eyes now. Bob had involuntarily put out his hand but Miss Gerald would not see it. Indeed, she turned farther from him, as if annoyed by Bob's persistence. Bob's hand fell to his side, he drew himself up.

"I am ready, sir," he said quietly to the monocle-man.

"Perhaps it would be as well if you accompanied us," observed the monocle-man to the hammer-thrower.

"Certainly." The other understood. Bob was strong and he might change his mind and be less lamblike before reaching his destination. "It's a disagreeable job at best," murmured the hammer-thrower, "but I suppose I ought to see it through."

"It's nice of you," said Miss Gerald in a low dull tone.

A moment Bob's eyes gleamed dangerously, then he seemed to realize the presence of Miss Gerald's other guests once more and his handsome blond head dropped. "I guess it's your turn," he said to the hammer-man.

Miss Dolly looked at the composed proud girl with the "heart of stone." The temperamental little thing's hands were tightly closed. Suddenly once more she bent over to whisper—this time viciously—to Miss Gerald. "He kisses beautifully," she breathed. "And—and I hate you!" Miss Gerald did not answer; nor did she turn to regard Bob who quietly moved away now with the monocle-man and the hammer-thrower.

CHAPTER XXII—A REAL BENEFACTOR

Bob, the hammer-thrower and the monocle-man together entered the little station-house in the village. It wasn't much of a lock-up, but it was big enough to hold Bob and a few others, one of whom had just been released as the trio of new-comers walked in. His eye fell on Bob.

"That's my man," he exclaimed excitedly. "That's my escaped patient."

"Yes, that's he!" affirmed a second voice—that of the commodore.

"Got him this time!" came jubilantly from another side of the bare room, and Bob gazing, with no show of emotion, in that direction, discovered Dickie and Clarence were there too.

"Put me in the padded cell, would you?" said the maniac-medico furiously. "I'll see where you go. Come on. The car is waiting. There won't be any window-bouquets this time, I promise you."

Bob didn't answer. He didn't much care what they said.

"I got Gee-gee on the phone," went on Dan viciously, "and she has it all down in black and white, she tells me. The legal light up there has attended to that. A parcel of outrageous falsehoods! The audacity of that girl, too! When I showed her the enormity of her conduct, she only gave a merry little laugh. Said she was terribly fond of me, the minx! And would I come and sit in the front row when she was a bright and scintillating star?"

"And she said Gid-up wanted to know if I wouldn't like to gaze upon that cute little freckle once more?" added Clarence in choked tones.

"And all that, on account of you!" exclaimed the commodore, throwing out his arms and looking at the culprit. Dickie didn't say anything at the moment. He only glared.

Bob regarded the three with lack-luster gaze. He felt little interest in them now.

"Take him away!" said Dan, breathing hard. "Or I may do him an injury."

"Give him what's coming to him," breathed Dickie hoarsely. "He's got my girl hypnotized."

"Come on," said the maniac-medico sternly to Bob. "Let's waste no more time."

"Hold on," spoke the monocle-man quietly. "You are a little premature, gentlemen."

"What do *you* want to butt in for?" demanded the commodore aggressively of the monocle-man.

"Mr. Bennett has accompanied me here as my prisoner. Am I not right?" Appealing to the hammer-thrower.

"Correct," said that gentleman regretfully.

"What's he been doing besides wrecking homes?" asked the commodore.

"A few articles of jewelry have been missing at Mrs. Ralston's," said the hammer-thrower in that same tone. "It's a very regrettable affair. Miss Gerald, for example, lost her ring and it was traced to Mr. Bennett."

Bob stood it patiently. He wondered if his day would ever come.

"So?— He's the merry little social-highwayman, is he?" observed Dan. "The best I can say is, don't make a hero of him. Give him some real, old-fashioned justice."

"I'm afraid I can't honestly extend my sympathy to you," remarked Clarence to Bob stiffly.

"I'm not sorry," said Dickie frankly. "I'm glad. Anyhow, Miss Dolly will despise you now." With a ring of triumph in his voice.

"No, she won't," observed Bob, breaking silence for the first time. "It was being what people think I am that made her fall in love with me." He didn't want Dickie to feel too good. He remembered that unsportsmanlike punch. "She's my dear jolly little pal," Bob went on, "and she wanted to occupy an adjoining cell."

Dickie went up to Bob. "I'd like to give you another," he said in his nastiest accents.

"Gentlemen! Gentlemen!" It was the voice of the man at the desk. Authority now spoke. Up to now, amazement had held authority tongue-tied. "The prisoner came quietly, Mr. Moriarity?" Authority knew, then, the monocle-man. Evidently the two had a secret understanding. "Has he confessed?" "Not as yet," said the monocle-man significantly.

"And I'm not going to," spoke up Bob succinctly to the magistrate. "I'm not guilty."

"Then who is?" asked the monocle-man.

"You've got your hand on his arm," said Bob in that same forcible manner. The time had come for him to assert himself, however ridiculous his affirmation might sound. Authority should have the truth. Bob blurted it out fearlessly, holding his head well up as he spoke. "You've got your hand on his arm," he repeated.

Mr. Moriarity's reply quite took their breath away, especially Bob's. "Guess you're right," he said promptly, and something bright gleamed in his hand. "Don't move," he said to the hammer-thrower.

"But aren't you going to lock *him* up at all?" asked the commodore in disappointed tones, indicating Bob, after the monocle-man had shown the hammer-thrower a warrant for his (the hammer-thrower's) arrest, and had, at the conclusion of certain formalities, caused that dazed and angry individual to be led away.

"I am certainly not going to lock Mr. Bennett up," laughed the monocle-man who was in the best of humors.

The coup seemed to him a lovely one. For months he had been on the trail of the hammer-thrower. He told Bob—as dazed and bewildered as the hammer-thrower by the unexpected turn of events—all about it later. He had certainly taken an artistic way to complete the affair. And later, not that night, Bob learned, too, that it was Miss Gerald herself who had suggested the way, she having inherited some of the managerial genius of her father. Maybe, she was not averse to Bob's suffering a little after the wholly-intolerable way he had comported himself toward her and others of her aunt's guests. Maybe cruelty had mingled somewhat with retaliation. Proud, regal young womanhood sometimes can be cruel. But Bob probably deserved all those twinges and pangs and mournful emotions she had caused him. No one certainly had ever talked to her as he had done.

"May I sit down?" said Bob at length to the magistrate. He felt rather tired.

Authority gave him permission to sit. "Well, if you're not going to lock him up," said that maniac-med., looking viciously at Bob, "I am."

"No, you're not," observed the monocle-man easily. "Mr. Bennett is my friend. He has helped me immensely in this affair. Had he not projected his rather impetuous personality into it, certain difficulties would not have been smoothed out so easily. He created a diversion which threw the prisoner, naturally deep and resourceful, somewhat off his guard. But for Mr. Bennett's whimsical and, at times, diverting conduct," with a smile at Bob, "my fight against him," nodding toward the cell, "might not have culminated quite so soon. So," he added to the enraged medico, "Mr. Bennett has my full moral support, and, I may say," touching the pocket into which he had returned that something bright, "my physical support as well."

"But what about the treatment I have received?" stormed the med. "Locked up like—?"

"You shouldn't have been prowling around. Anyhow, I shall advise my good friend, Mr. Bennett, that should you seek to annoy him further, or to lay a single finger on him, he will have an excellent case for damages. I can explain away a great deal that is inexplicable to the rest of you, and that explanation will serve fully to rehabilitate Mr. Bennett in the esteem of certain people as a not unnormal person. How far I can restore his popularity," with a laugh, "is another matter."

Bob stared straight ahead. "How did you do it?" he said to the monocle-man. "What made you certain?"

"I saw him place the ring in your pocket. Feel here," walking over to Bob. The latter felt where the other indicated. "A little vest-pocket camera!" said the monocle-man softly. "I photographed the act— the outstretched hand with the ring in it!—you, unsuspecting, half sprawling over the green felt of the table! your coat tails inviting the ring—Besides, one of my men took the place of that outside-operator and received a certain little article of jewelry that night you came blundering back to Mrs. Ralston's. We nabbed the outside-operator and—well, he's told certain things." With satisfaction. "We have, in short, a clear case."

Bob held his head. "It's whirling," he said. "I'll get some things straightened out after a little, I suppose."

"That's right," observed the monocle-man.

"There are some things you can't straighten out," said Dan in an ugly tone. "This is all very well for you, but what about us?"

Just at that moment there was a flutter of skirts at the door.

Gee-gee and Gid-up came in, the former in a state of great agitation.

"How dared you?" she gasped, going up to the monocle-man and standing with arms akimbo.

"Send you that note, commanding your presence here?" said the monocle-man. "I dared, my dear," he added slowly, "because I hold the cards."

"Don't you 'dear' me," she retorted stormily.

"I wouldn't, seriously," he returned. "It might be dangerous. Women like you are dangerous, you know. I fancy our friends here," glancing toward the commodore and Clarence, "have found that out.

But it will be a lesson. 'We'll never wander more from our own fireside,'" he hummed.

"Well," said Gee-gee, shaking her auburn tresses, "those were pretty bold statements of what you could do to me, in that note you sent."

"They were true, my dear."

The green eyes flared. Gee-gee was shaking all over. Gid-up looked rather frightened.

"Take it easy," said the monocle-man.

"I'd like to see you prove what you can do," she returned. "You say I have framed-up a lot of false-hoods—a tissue of lies—in that affidavit the lawyer at Mrs. Ralston's drew up. I tell you they're all true." Dan looked weak. "Everything I've told happened just at I said it did, and he knows it." Pointing a finger at the commodore.

"I wonder if I ought not to put you in jail now?" said the monocle-man meditatively. "There's a cell vacant next to the hammer-thrower. You would be congenial spirits."

"It's proofs I'm asking, Mr. Detective," retorted Gee-gee, apparently not greatly abashed by this threat. She was accustomed to hitting back.

"Yes, it's proofs," said Gid-up, but in weaker accents.

The monocle-man shook a reproving finger at Gid-up. "You're in bad company, my dear," he observed. "You're out of Gee-gee's class. You're just trying to be in it."

"I don't want any of your impertinence," answered Gid-up with a faint imitation of Gee-gee's manner. "He's a proper bad one." Pointing to Clarence who presented a picture of abject misery. "And when I tell all the things he done to me—"

"But you won't tell them."

"I have." Defiantly. "In that paper the lawyer drew up."

"But you're going to sign a little paper I have here, repudiating all that," he answered her.

"Oh, am I?" Elevating her turned-up nose.

"You are." Blandly.

"Guess again," said Gid-up saucily.

"You can't prove what we told in that affidavit isn't true," reaffirmed Gee-gee. Only she and Gid-up could know it was a "frame-up"; they had builded carefully and were sure of their ground. "We know our rights and we're going to have them. We're not afraid of you."

"Then why are you here?" quietly.

"That lawyer at the house said we might as well see you, just to call your bluff. He said, since we had told the truth, we had nothing to fear."

"I don't think you're quite so confident as you seem," observed the monocle-man. "My note awoke a little uneasiness, or you wouldn't be here. This young lady," turning to Gid-up, "suffered a mild case of stage fright, if I am any judge of human nature."

"Me?" said Gid-up. "I defy you."

"Here's the answer," replied the monocle-man, taking another paper from his pocket.

"What's that?" said Gee-gee scornfully. "I suppose it's some lies from him." Alluding to the commodore. "The lawyer told me to be prepared for them."

"No; it isn't that. It's only a stenographic report of a conversation you and your friend had together in your room, the night you arrived at Mrs. Ralston's."

"A stenographic report? Nonsense!" Sharply. Gee-gee remembered all about that conversation. "How could you—"

"There's a dictograph in the room you occupied, my dear," observed the monocle-man.

"A dic—" Gee-gee seemed to turn green. "Good Gawd!" she said.

It wasn't very long thereafter that Gee-gee and Gid-up departed.

"Back to the old life!" said Gee-gee wearily. "And just when I thought my ambition to be a star was coming true."

"Life is sure tough," observed Gid-up, abandoning her society manner.

"I'm sick of the whole thing. Got a mind to jump in the river."

"Gas for me!" from poor Gid-up wearily.

"No, you won't. And I won't. We'll just go on. Lord! how long."

"Anyhow, that detective promised to introduce us to a real Russian grand duke who's in old New York. Maybe we can get in the papers on that."

"Perhaps." More thoughtfully from Gee-gee. "It wasn't so worse of the detective to promise that, after he'd got us down and walked on us."

"You must make dukie drink out of your slipper," suggested Gid-up. "The detective said he was mad after beautiful stage girls. Grand dukes always are." Hopefully. "And if you do make him do that, it would be heralded from coast to coast."

"It's as good as done," said Gee-gee confidently. "It'll prove me a great actress, sure." In a brighter tone.

"I always said you had talent," remarked Gid-up.

"Cheese it," retorted Gee-gee elegantly. "Ain't you the fond flatterer!"

"Anyhow, I'm glad I don't have to do society talk any more," said Gid-up, and stuck a piece of gum in her mouth.

"Yes," said Gee-gee, "my jaws is most broke."

"Maybe you'd better tighten up your hobble a little for dukie," suggested Gid-up.

"Have to stand still the rest of my life if I did," observed Gee-gee, swishing along about six inches a step.

"You could divide it a little."

"So I could."

By this time they had forgotten about the river, or taking gas. The duke had already become a real person in their lives and they talked on, devising stunts for his Vivacious Greatness. By this time, too, the monocle-man seemed to them a real benefactor.

Meanwhile the "real benefactor" had been reading from that stenographic report to Dan and the others. The commodore nearly jumped out of his boots for joy.

"Read that again," he said.

The monocle-man, reading: "'This ain't half bad enough. You think up something now, Gee-gee.'

"'Doping a poor little thing is always good stuff to spring on a jury, Gid-up. And you could make yourself up young with your hair done up in a pigtail, with a cute little baby-blue bow on the end.'

"'But that sounds old, Gee-gee. You can sure invent something new—'" etc., etc.

The monocle-man finished reading and laid down the paper. "There you are, gentlemen," he observed in a lively tone. "The stenographers will swear to that. They were dressed as house-maids, but at night and on certain occasions, they used one of the rooms Mrs. Ralston placed at my disposal as an office. When I came down here I didn't expect to be involved in a domestic drama. It rather forced itself upon me. It came as part of the day's work. I overheard your conversation with Miss Dolly that night." Significantly to Bob. That young gentleman flushed.

"I have taken the liberty of destroying the report of that conversation, I may add. Miss Dolly is charming." With a smile. "I, also, had a record of your conversation with these three gentlemen"—indicating Dan, Clarence and Dickie—"after they entered your room one night, via the trellis and the window. That conversation introduced me into the domestic drama. I became an actor in it whether I would or not. But for my whispered instructions to one of my assistants in the garden, you three gentlemen would have been arrested." Dan stared at Clarence in momentary consternation. "You did not need the golf-club because my man removed the dog."

"It seems," said Dan effusively to the monocle-man, "you have been our good angel. If any remuneration—?"

"No," answered the monocle-man. "What I have done for you was only incidental and my reward was the enjoyment I got out of the affair—in watching how the threads crossed and recrossed, and how they tangled and untangled. It was better than going to a show. It made work a pleasure. Besides, I shall be well rewarded for what I have accomplished in another direction." Looking toward the cell.

"I tried to get him in England and failed. In France, the story was the same. He is rather a remarkable personality. A born criminal and an actor, as well! Of good family, he wedged his way into society, through the all-round amateur athletic route. He was generally well liked." Bob thought of Miss Gerald and looked down. He couldn't help wondering if she would not greatly have preferred his (Bob's) occupying that cell, instead of the other man who had seemed to interest her so much.

"Now for Mrs. Dan," observed the commodore, jubilantly waving the stenographic report. "This will bring her to time."

"And my wife, too!" said Clarence with equal joy.

"I thought I would save you gentlemen some trouble and so have already placed the report in the ladies' hands," said the monocle-man affably. "Indeed, they came to me afterward and told me they had been shamefully deceived. Mrs. Dan looked as if she had had a good cry—from joy, no doubt. Mrs. Clarence's voice was tremulous. Same cause, I am sure. I think you will find them contrite and anxious to make up."

"This is great," said Dan.

"Glorious!" observed Clarence.

"Think of it! No public disgrace!"

"No being held up as monsters in the press!"

"It's too good to be true." The commodore threw out his arms and advanced toward the monocle-man.

But the latter waved him away. "Save your embraces for your wives," he observed.

"I love all the world," said Dan.

"Me, too!" from Clarence.

"I presume I am free to take my departure, gentlemen?" said Bob, rising.

"You are free as the birds of the air for all of me," answered the monocle-man.

"Hold on one moment," begged the commodore. "No; I'm not going to detain you forcibly. As a friend I ask you to wait." Bob paused. "I'm a good fellow," said Dan effusively, "and I don't wish the world harm. I don't want you to go wandering around any more as you are. Why, you're a regular Frankenstein. You're an iron automaton that goes about trampling on people. After all I've gone through, I have charity toward others. I won't have you treading on people's finer sensibilities and smashing connubial peace and comfort all to splinters."

"But what can I do?" suggested Bob. He meant the three weeks weren't yet up.

"Here's what I propose to Clarence and Dickie. I see now you'll win, anyhow. You've got the grit and the nerve. So as long as we have simply got to pay in the end, why not do so at once and so spare others? That'll be the way I'll pay him." Alluding to the monocle-man. "It's my way of showing my gratitude for what he's done. And now I think of it, I can't see that I ought to blame you so much, Bob, for all that has transpired."

"Oh, you don't?" With faint irony.

"No; you only did what you had to, and maybe we were a little rough. Forget it." The commodore extended his hand.

The act melted Bob. He took it. "Good friends, once more!" chirped Dan, and extended an arm to include Clarence. "You've won. The money's fairly yours, Bob. Only as a personal favor, I ask you to be, at once, as you were. Be your old natural self immediately."

"I'll pay my share to have him that way again," said Clarence heartily. "I want to spare the world too. Besides, he's won all right enough."

"It's three weeks or nothing from me," said Dickie. "You chaps may want to spare the world, but I don't want to spare him."

"I'll pay for Dickie," replied good old Dan. "And gladly!"

Dickie shrugged. Dan wrote out a check. "Congratulations!" he said. "And for us, too!" Turning to Clarence. "Think of the thousands in alimony it might have cost us!"

"We've simply got to call a halt on old Bob," said Clarence fervently. "Bet's off! We lose."

Bob took the check. "I believe I am entitled to it, for I certainly would have stuck it out now. I am sure I wouldn't do it all over again, though, for ten times the amount. Nevertheless, I thank you." He shook himself. "Free! Isn't it great? Will you do something for me?" To the monocle-man.

"Gladly," was the reply. "I was secretly informed of that wager of yours and I was immensely interested in your little social experiment. You see I make my living by prevarication and subterfuges. And that"—with a laugh—"is more than a man can make by telling the truth. It's a wicked world. Fraud and humbug are trumps."

"What I want you to do," said Bob, ignoring this homily, "is to express my grip to New York. Also, tell Miss Gerald that I've gone and kindly thank Mrs Ralston and Miss Gerald for asking me down."

"Why don't you thank them yourself?"

"I think they would be more pleased if I complied with the formalities by proxy."

"Shall I add you had a charming time?"

"You may use your own judgment."

Bob walked to the door.

"I guess it's I who am crazy," said the maniac-doctor, again waking up.

CHAPTER XXIII—MAKING GOOD

Bob sent dad a modest-sized check the next day. "Result of hustling," he wrote. "Spend freely. There'll be more coming presently." Then Bob went down on the narrow road that isn't straight, but that has a crook in it. He stopped somewhere near the crook, and entering an office greeted a melancholy-looking man who had "bad business" and "country going to pot" written all over his face. The melancholy man was a club acquaintance.

"What's the most abused and worst thing on the street that isn't straight?" said Bob debonairly.

"That's right. Call us names," replied the melancholy man with a sigh. "Everybody's doing it."

"Have you got something so awful people turn their heads away when you speak of it?"

"There's the Utopian," observed the other. "Only a buzzard would get near it."

"Do they call the promoter a thief?"

"They do."

"And is he crazy?"

"He is. It's either jail or a lunatic asylum for him."

Bob handed what was left of the commodore's check to the melancholy man. "Buy Utopian," he said.

"All right," answered the melancholy man listlessly. He was beyond feeling any emotion.

"I believe in Utopian," observed Bob. "I have here," touching his forehead, "inside information that it is an excellent little railroad property."

"Oh, it isn't a railroad," said the melancholy man. "It's—"

"Don't tell me what it is," retorted Bob. "Repeat some of those things the world calls the promoter."

The melancholy man was obliging.

"Heavens! He must be an awful honest man!" said Bob and started toward the door, where he turned. "Pyramid with the profits." And Bob walked out.

That afternoon he went to a real-estate man and asked where he could lease a small factory. While at college he had invented a small appliance for automobiles, which he felt sure was good and would commend itself to manufacturers. Bob knew about all there was to know about a car. After he had looked at several old deserted buildings on the outskirts, any one of which might answer his purpose, Bob strolled into a number of automobile agencies near Columbus Square, and showed them his little patent. The men in charge were willing to express an opinion; several appeared interested. Of course, Bob would ultimately have to go to the "higher-ups," but he wanted first to find out what these practical chaps thought. One of them even asked Bob if he wanted a partner? Bob didn't. He had all the capital needed, he replied.

He was taking a serious sober view of life now. He felt himself no longer "darn fool Bob," or careless Bob, or lazy Bob. He might have done something with his little device long ago, but he had forgotten all about it. Its creation had been a passing whim. Bob really had a good head for machinery though, and now he was beginning to feel out his path. He wanted to work hard, too, which was a novel sensation. It felt, also, like a permanent sensation. Meeting several chaps, he refused their invitations to partake of the sparkling, much to their surprise, as heretofore he had been a prince of good fellows. Henceforth, however, he was going to be king of himself.

That night, in the old home, in the old square, Dolly called him up by telephone.

"How *could* you disappoint me so!" said jolly little pal. "The idea of your just pretending to be a burglar."

"Me, pretend?" Bob laughed. "I say, that's good. Didn't I tell you all along I wasn't?"

"But why didn't you *make* me believe you weren't?" retorted little pal reproachfully. "To think of your deceiving me like that!"

"Deceive you? That's good, too. Why, I told you again and again I was just a plain ordinary person. You were just bound to idealize me!"

There was a brief pause. "Are you so disappointed in me, you are going to disown me now?" continued Bob.

"No-a. I'm still your jolly little pal. Only to think though, there never was a chance for those adjoining cells, after all!"

"Well, there seemed a good chance, anyhow."

"Yes, it was nice and exciting while it lasted." The temperamental little thing sighed. "It's awful humdrum up here now."

Bob didn't ask any questions about the people up there. "You ought to have fallen in love with the hammer-thrower," he said. "He was the real thing."

"I suppose I should have," she seemed to agree. "Wasn't I stupid? Never mind. Say something nice."

"Like you," said Bob.

"Heaps? I need cheering."

"Heaps."

"Much obliged. You're awfully good. What are you doing this evening?"

"I was sitting by the fire in dad's old-fashioned den, thinking and dreaming."

"All alone?"

"Entirely."

"What were you thinking of?"

"Machinery. And a factory."

"And will it have a tall chimney that belches smoke?"

"I trust ultimately to attain to the kind of a chimney you refer to. At present, I shall have to content myself with a comparatively insignificant one. I have visions of a chimney four hundred feet high some day."

"Belching ugly smoke?"

"It won't look ugly to me. It'll look blissful."

The biggest sigh of all quivered from afar. "Another dream shattered! My! but I'm growing up fast. I feel a million years old. Anyhow, I'll never marry Dickie."

"Wouldn't if I were you. He doesn't fight fair. Before he got through he'd have all your dad's chimneys, as well as his own, and then he'd put you on an allowance. You'd have to account for every pin and needle you bought."

"Yes; I know. When I do find the right man I'll bring him to you and let you pass in judgment. You shall tell me whether I can or can't."

"All right—though isn't that rather a paternal prerogative?"

"Oh, dad always lets me do what I want. You're the only man that has ever dared oppose me."

"But suppose I did oppose you in a matter of such importance?"

Miss Dolly thought. "We won't cross that bridge before we come to it. You said you were thinking *and* dreaming. I know what you were thinking about. Now, what were you dreaming about all by your lonely, sitting by the fire?"

Bob was glad he didn't have to blurt out the truth any more. He evaded. "Did I say dreaming?" he asked.

"You did. Was it of some one?"

"Pooh! What nonsense!"

"Oh, it isn't nonsense to do that."

"I was only thinking of chimneys and things like that," returned Bob. That was an out-and-outer. He shuddered to think of the answer he would have had to make a few days ago.

"Never mind," said the jolly little pal. "You needn't tell me. There are some things we keep locked up, forever and ever, in the inner sanctums of our hearts, aren't there?" Sadly. "And we die and they are buried with us. Oh, dear! I'm beginning to feel dreadful. Only jolly little pal is awfully sorry." For him, she meant. Bob winced. "I hate to think of you sitting there, poor dear, all alone, and—and—"

"I'm having a bully time—honest," said Bob. "I really am. I'm planning out my future. I'm going to do something. I'm tired of being nothing. I'll work right with the workmen at first."

"And you will be all perspirey and covered with soot?" In horror.

"I'll be worse than that. I'll be sweaty and covered with soot," said Bob practically.

Dolly groaned. "It seems to me as if everything is upside down."

"No. Downside down. 'Life is real; life is earnest,'" he quoted, laughing.

"Oh, dear! That solemn sound! I can tell you are terribly determined." He did not answer. "Well, good-by, great, big, perspirey—I mean sweaty, sooty old pal!"

"Good-by, Dolly. And thank you for calling me up. It did me good to hear little pal's voice. Wish me luck."

"I'll send you a horseshoe to-morrow," she laughed. And then suddenly, as an afterthought— "By the way, I have a 'fession to make."

"All right. 'Fess ahead."

"Well, I don't suppose I really and truly—deep down, you know— actually ever did quite think you were a regular burglar. I guess it was the dramatic situation that appealed to me. I've often thought I had 'histrionic ability' and you did make such a big, bold, handsome, darling make-believe burglar to play with, I just couldn't resist."

"I understand!" said Bob. "I guess—deep down—I guessed as much." And rang off.

Bob went back to the fireplace. Was he dreaming now or only thinking? Dolly's voice had taken him back to Mrs. Ralston's, and the coals now framed a face. He looked quickly from them, his eyes following the smoke of his pipe. But the smoke now framed the face. Bob half-closed his eyes an instant, then resolutely he laid down his pipe and went to bed. Dad had closed the rather spacious old-fashioned house when he went away, and a momentary feeling of loneliness assailed Bob, as he realized there was no other person in the place, but he fought it down. Work was his incentive now—hard work—

The next day he learned they had lodged the promoter in jail. The big men had gone gunning for him, and, as usual, they got him. They got the "Utopian," too. They took that because there wasn't anything else to take. Incidentally, they discredited the broker's statement that no one but a buzzard would go near it. Or, maybe, some of the big men were buzzards in disguise. Anyhow, they had the Utopian on their hands, and after they had settled with the promoter who had dared cross the trail of the big interests in his operations, they poked their fingers into Utopian and prodded it and examined it more carefully and discovered that with "honest judicial management" and a proper application of more funds that which had been but an odorous prospect might be converted into a "property." The promoter had taken funds which he shouldn't so he was out of their way, until he got pardoned.

The Utopian accordingly now began to soar. There were plenty of people who would sniff at it in its new aspect, and take a bite, too. A shoal of speculators wanted to get aboard. That "honest management" was a bait; that "property" probability became a "sure thing." Big names were juggled in little offices. The usual thing happened—just one of those common occurrences hardly worth describing—only later it would probably be included in a congressional investigation and there would be a few reverberations at Albany. Bob pulled out in about two days.

"How'd you know?" said the broker.

"Fellow feeling. Been called a thief and a crazy man, myself."

"What you want to buy now? The next rankest thing I know of is—"

Bob shook his head. "Never again. Good-by forever."

"Good-by," said the melancholy man. He thought he would see Bob down there again some day, but he never did. Bob went to a bank and opened an account. He wasn't exactly rich but he had a nice comfortable feeling. Moreover he expected to build solidly. He leased the factory and then he went to work. Dad came home. He didn't seem much interested in what Bob was doing. He loafed around and told fish stories. Bob got up about five a.m. but dad didn't arise until nine. Sometimes he had his breakfast in bed and had his man bring him the newspaper. Bob didn't have a man, though he soon began to prosper. The device was considered necessary in the trade; it proved practical.

Bob added to his factory and built a fair-sized chimney. Dreamily he wondered if it would realize jolly little chum's idea of a chimney. He had to cut out all the social functions now for he was so tired when he got home he wanted only his dinner and his pipe and bed. Dad, however, stayed out late. He remarked once he thought he would learn to tango. Bob never knew though whether he carried out the idea or not.

The newspapers, a few months later, apprised Bob that Gee-gee had landed the grand duke. A snapshot revealed him imbibing from Gee-gee's Cinderella slipper. Possibly the grand duke was enraged over the snap-shot. More likely, however, he didn't care; he was so high up he could do anything and snap his fingers at the world. Bob permitted himself a little recreation; out of mild curiosity, he went to see Gee-gee. She now had a fair-sized part and was talked about. Incidentally, she had acquired a few additional wriggles.

His Vivacious Highness sat in a box and Gee-gee wriggled mostly for him. She hardly looked at the audience, but the audience didn't act offended. It applauded. Gee-gee's dream had come true. She was a star. And to her credit she reached out a helping hand to Gid-up. The latter now said more than "Send for the doctor." She had eight lines—which was certainly getting on some. Bob, however, didn't notice Dan or Clarence in the audience. They were probably billing and cooing at home now. Only grand dukes can afford to toy with Gee-gees. Bob didn't stay to see and hear it all for a little of Gee-gee went a long way, and besides, he had to get up early. Dad though, who accompanied Bob, said he would stay right through.

Once on Fifth Avenue, Bob passed Miss Gerald; she was just getting out of her car. An awful temptation seized him to stop, but he managed to suppress it, for he had himself fairly in hand by this time. He saw they would almost meet, but there were many people and, in the press, he didn't have to see her. So he didn't. He felt sure she would cut him if he did. It was the first foolish thing he had done for some time; he realized that when he got away. But what was he to do? He objected to being cut, and by her, of all persons. He regretted the incident very much. It hurt his pride and, of course, he had earned her dislike.

Bob hied him factoryward and toiled mightily that day. It was work—work—though to what end? If he only knew! He had tried to tell himself that he was learning to forget, that he was becoming reconciled to the inevitable, but that quick glimpse he had caught of her from a distance, before he drifted by with the others, had set his pulses tingling. For a moment now Bob gave way to dreaming; the day was almost done. He sat with his head on his hand and his elbow on the desk. He had shown he was more than a dancing man. He would now have to fight an even harder battle. He would have to take her out of his heart and mind.

But he couldn't do that. It was impossible, when his whole nature clamored for her. He yielded now to the dubious luxury of thinking of her. He hoped he wouldn't see her again and then gradually he would win in that fight against nature—or do his best to. Yes; he must do his best; he must, he repeated to himself, closing a firm hand resolutely. Then he started and stared—at a vision standing before him.

"Why did you cut me to-day?"

CHAPTER XXIV—AT THE PORTALS

It was some time before Bob recovered sufficiently to answer. Fortunately they were alone in Bob's private office. From below came the sound of hammers, but that and the dingy surroundings did not seem to disconcert her. She looked at Bob coldly, the violet eyes full of directness.

"I—well, I feared you would cut me," stammered Bob. "Won't—won't you sit down?"

"No, thank you. At least, not yet. I," accusingly, "am not accustomed to being cut, and if any of my friends cut me, I want to know why. That's why I am here."

She was her father's daughter at that moment—straight, forceful.

"But," said Bob eagerly, looking once more the way he used to, before he had got into this sobering business of manufacturer, "that's just the point. You see I felt I had somehow forfeited my right to be one of your friends. I felt out of the pale."

"Do you think you deserve to forfeit the right?"

"I—perhaps. I don't know. I'm very confused about all that happened at your aunt's place."

Was that the shadow of a smile on the proud lips? Bob wasn't looking at her. He dared not. He was talking to a drawing of his device.

"Perhaps you have heard of that confounded wager," he went on. "I told you why I—I didn't want to see you. At least, I think I did."

"I have a vague impression of something of the kind," said the girl.

"And there you are," observed Bob helplessly. "It was an awful muddle, all right. You certainly punished me some, though. Honestly, if I offended you, you did get back good and hard."

"Did I?" said she tentatively. "Is that a drawing of it on the wall?" She was looking at the device.

"Yes. That's what I make."

"Won't you show me around?"

Bob did, walking as in a dream among the dingy workmen who paused as the vision passed. For a long time they talked—just plain ordinary talk. Then he told her how he was inventing something else and Miss Gerald listened while all differences seemed magically to have dropped between them. Drinking deep of the joy of the moment, Bob yielded to the unadulterated happiness that went with being near her. He forgot all about the long future when he would see her no more.

Finally Miss Gerald got up to go. They had returned to Bob's office and she had seated herself in a shabby old chair.

Bob's face fell. His heart had been beating fast and the old light had come to his eyes.

"Going?" he said awkwardly.

"Yes."

She put out her hand and Bob took it, looking into her eyes. Then— he never knew how it happened—he had her in his arms. Bang! bang! went Bob's hammers below and they seemed to be competing with the beating of his heart. At length the girl stirred slightly. She was wonderful in her proud compliance to Bob's somewhat chaotic and over-powering expression of his emotions. "I suffered, too, a little, perhaps," she said.

That nearly completed Bob's undoing. "You! you!" he said, holding her from him and regarding her face eagerly, devouringly.

"Yes," the proud lips curled a little, "I haven't really a heart of stone, you know."

Then Bob became chaotic once more for it was as if heaven had been hurled at him. He spoke burning words of truth and this time they did not get him into trouble. She drank them all in, too. Then he began to ask questions in that same chaotic manner. He was so masterful she had to answer.

"Yes, yes," she said, "of course, I do."

"When did it begin?"

"A long, long time ago."

"You have loved me a long time?" he exulted and drew a deep breath. "A moment ago I was pondering on the problems of life and wondering what was the use of it all? Now—" He paused.

"Now?" said the girl and her eyes were direct and clear. The love light in them—for it was that—shone as the light of stars.

Bob threw out his arms. "Life is great," he said.

A moment they stood apart and looked at each other. "It can't be," said Bob. "It is too much to believe. I certainly must prove it once more."

"One moment," said Miss Gerald. "Dolly told me you kissed her."

"I did."

"Why, if as you say, it was only I—?"

Bob was silent.

"Did—did she ask you to?"

Bob did not answer.

"You don't answer?" The violet eyes studied him discerningly.

"All I can say is I did kiss her." He would not betray jolly little pal.

The violet eyes looked satisfied. "You have answered," she said. "I think I understand the situation thoroughly."

Bob impetuously wanted to demonstrate once more that she was really she—that it wasn't a dream—but she held him back and looked into his eyes. "You've said a good many things," said Miss Gerald. "But there's one you haven't."

"What?"

"It's one you really ought to ask, after all this demonstration."

"Oh!" said Bob loudly. "Will you marry me?"

"Yes," she answered. And for the first time voluntarily offered him her lips.

Suddenly the sound of hammers stopped.

"What's happening?" she asked.

"Closing time. May I see you to your car?"

"Yes," she laughed, "if you will get in."

"I'll get in if you won't be ashamed of having a rather dingy-looking individual by your side?"

"I'm proud of you, Bob," said her father's daughter. "And I believe in you."

"And—?" he suggested.

"I love you," she said simply.

Bob tried to say something, but words didn't seem to come. Then silently he opened the door and they passed out. He helped her in the car and held a small gloved hand all the way down Fifth Avenue. Young people who can be cruel are, also, capable of going to the other extreme. It wasn't Fifth Avenue for Bob. It was Paradise.

Dad heard the news that night. "Of course," he said. "I expected it." Then, with a twinkle of the eye. "But I'm glad you got started in life for yourself first, son. I was afraid you would ask her before you had the right."

"You afraid? Then you did suggest my doing it, just to try me, to see what kind of stuff I was made of? I thought so. I told her so." Bob's eyes now began to twinkle. "Sure that's all you did, dad, to find out if I was a real man or a sawdust one?"

"Perhaps I did misrepresent slightly the state of the parental exchequer. As a matter of fact, I'm still pretty well off, Bob. Though they did bounce me a little, I was not so much ruined as I let people think. I didn't deny those bankruptcy stories, because I wanted you to make good, dear boy. And you have!" There was pride and affection in dad's tones. "But now that you have, there will be no further need to continue that Japanese custom. I have ample for my simple needs and a little left over to go fishing with."

Bob might have protested, but just at that moment a car swung in front of the house, where it stopped. On the back seat sat a lady. The driver got out and started up the steps to dad's house. By this time Bob was coming down the steps. He hastened to the lady.

"So good of you!" he said, his eyes alight. "I ordered to-day that car of my own," he added, leaning over the door.

"Are you sure you can afford it yet?" she laughed.

"Sure. And it will be a beauty. As fit for you as any car could be!"

"Are you going like that—hatless?" she asked.

"I—well, I was wondering if I couldn't induce you to come in for a moment?" Eagerly. "Want you to meet dad. Or shall I bring him out here?"

"I'll go in, of course," she said, rising at once. "And I shall be very glad."

"He—he was only trying me out, after all," spoke Bob as he opened the door of the car. "That advice, I mean. You remember? And he pretended to be broke, too, just to test me. He told me just now."

"I think I shall like your father," said Miss Gerald.

"Oh, we're bully chums!"

By this time they were in the house. Bob took her by the hand and led her to dad.

"I remember your mother and I knew your father," said dad, when Bob had presented him. "Your mother was very beautiful."

Gwendoline thanked him, while Bob gazed upon her with adoring eyes.

"Isn't she wonderful, dad?" he said.

"Wonderful, indeed," said dad fondly, a little sadly. Perhaps he was thinking of the time when his own bride had stood right there, in the home he had bought for her. Perhaps he saw her eyes with the light of love in them—eyes long since closed. "I trust you will not think me trite if I say, God bless you," murmured dad.

"I won't think you trite at all," said Gwendoline Gerald, approaching nearer to dad. "I think it very nice."

"And would you think me trite if I—?"

Dad's meaning was apparent for Gwendoline's golden head bent toward him and dad's lips just brushed the fair brow.

"I'm very glad. I think Bob will make a good husband. He will have to set himself a high mark though, to deserve you, my dear."

"That's just what I keep telling her myself," observed Bob. He experienced anew a touch of that chaotic feeling but didn't give way to it on account of dad's being there.

"Don't set the mark too high, or you may leave me far behind," laughed Gwendoline Gerald. "By the way I've asked Dolly to be first bridesmaid and she has consented. Said she supposed that was the 'next best thing,' though I can't imagine what she meant."

"That's jolly," said Bob. He thrilled at these little delicious details of the approaching event. "But I suppose we should be going now."

"Is it the opera?" asked dad.

Bob answered that it was. "She insisted on coming for me in her car," he laughed. "Would have had one myself now if I had imagined anything like this. It was rather sudden, you know."

"It looks as if I made him do it," said the girl with a laugh. "I went right to his office, and that, after his refusing me once, when I proposed to him."

"Did you do that, Bob?"

"Well, I didn't believe she meant it. Did you?" To Miss Gerald.

"That's telling," said Gwendoline, and looked so inviting in that wonderful opera costume, so white and tall and alluring, so many other things calculated to fire a young man's soul, that Bob had difficulty not to resort to extreme masculine measures to make her tell.

"Hope you have a pleasant evening," observed dad politely as they went out together, a couple the neighbors might well find excuse to stare at.

"Oh, I guess we'll manage to pull through," said Bob.

Their first evening out all alone by themselves in great, big gay New York! It was nice and shadowy, too, in the big limousine where the dim light spiritualized the girl's beauty.

"Tell now," he urged, "what I asked you in there?"

"Did I mean it?" Her starry eyes met his. "Perhaps a little bit. But I'm glad you didn't accept. I'm glad it came out the other way," she laughed.

Bob forgot there was a possibility of some one peering in and seeing them. Those laughing lips were such a tremendous lure. Then they both sat very still. Wheels sang around them; there was magic in the air.

"Just think of it!" said Bob with sudden new elation.

"What?"

"Why, there'll be nights and nights like this," he said, as if he had made an important new discovery.

"And 'then some'!" added the classical young goddess non-classically and gaily, as they turned into the Great White Way.

THE END

By FREDERIC S. ISHAM

The Strollers. Illustrated by Harrison Fisher. 12mo, Cloth, $1.50

Under the Rose. Illustrated by Howard Chandler Christy, 12mo, Cloth, $1.50

Black Friday. Illustrated by Harrison Fisher, 12mo, Cloth, $1.50

The Lady of the Mount. Illustrated by Lester Ralph, 12mo, Cloth, $1.50

Half a Chance. Illustrated by Herman Pfeifer, 12mo, Cloth, $1.50

The Social Buccaneer. Illustrated by W. B. King, 12mo, Cloth, $1.50

A Man and His Money. Illustrated by Max J. Spero, 12mo, Cloth, $1.25 Net

Aladdin from Broadway. Illustrated by William Thatcher Van Dresser, 12mo, Cloth, $1.25 Net

Im The Story

personalised classic books

UNIQUE GIFT

FOR KIDS, PARTNERS
AND FRIENDS

Timeless books such as:

Alice in Wonderland · The Jungle Book · The Wonderful Wizard of Oz
Peter and Wendy · Robin Hood · The Prince and The Pauper
The Railway Children · Treasure Island · A Christmas Carol

Romeo and Juliet · Dracula

Highly Customizable   **Change** Books Title   **Replace** Characters Names with yours   **Upload** Photo for inside pages   **Add** Inscriptions

Visit
Im The Story .com
and order yours today!

CPSIA information can be obtained
at www.ICGtesting.com
Printed in the USA
BVHW05s0612180618
519085BV00014B/91/P